The Practical Guide to Stop Overthinking & Fix Your Relationships

Let Go of Toxic Thoughts, Overcome Anxiety & Build Connection, Intimacy & Trust with Your Partner

First published by Tricycle Games Inc. 2025

Let Go, Heal, Grow & Love: A Self-Help Book Series About Letting Go of the Past, Thinking Clearly, and Loving Without Fear - Book Two

First edition

ISBN (paperback): 978-1-0689029-5-6
ISBN (hardcover): 978-1-0689029-7-0

This book was professionally typeset on Reedsy.
Find out more at reedsy.com

For Barbara, my sister, whose brilliance and kindness inspires me.

Contents

Introduction

You're going to regret this, the voice in my head whispered as I boarded my flight alone.

The empty seat beside me was a loud reminder I wasn't ready to face.

Just weeks earlier, that seat was supposed to be occupied by my girlfriend, and we were to be headed to South America to tour the Galapagos Islands. Flights booked. Hotels reserved. Dreams mapped out.

There were no dramatic goodbyes, no storming out of the room like we see in the movies. Just a slow, silent fade. Unanswered messages. Vague responses. The kind of emotional retreat that leaves you staring at your phone, analyzing every text, every interaction, wondering where things went wrong.

I should have seen the red flags flapping in my recently divorced wind. The whirlwind romance, the age gap, and my emotional healing not yet complete.

So, I got on the plane alone. I was embarking on a year-long journey that would take me across three continents, punctuated by breathtaking views, new experiences, and—

most of all—nonstop overthinking.

Every new destination brought the same old questions. I continued to ask myself: *Why did she leave? What could I have done differently? What was wrong with me?*

I dated other people. I met incredible, interesting, beautiful humans. But instead of being present, I was stuck in the past—comparing, analyzing, and replaying every scene like a bad director obsessed with reshooting an old film. The fear of another unexplained exit haunted every coffee date and late-night conversation.

And that's the real problem with overthinking in relationships: It pulls you out of the present and plants you in a version of reality that doesn't even exist anymore. Or maybe never did.

But here's what I've learned: While you're busy overthinking one chapter, life is already writing you a better one.

Why This Book? Why Now?

If you've picked up this book, I'm guessing you know exactly what it feels like to be stuck in an overthinking loop about a relationship. Maybe you analyze every message. Maybe you obsess over what you should have said—or shouldn't have said. Maybe you've been burned by a past relationship and now question every new one, looking for warning signs even where none exist.

I see you, and I want to meet you where you are.

Research tells us that as many as 73% of 25- to 35-year-olds and 52% of 45- to 55-year-olds struggle with overthinking (Camacho, 2024). It's not just you—it's a human thing. But just because it's common doesn't mean it has to control your life.

This book is here to help you break free.

This isn't just a book about overthinking—it's about reclaiming your peace, your confidence, and your relationships.

We'll take a deep dive into understanding why we overthink, especially when it comes to love, dating, and relationships. You'll learn about the psychology behind overthinking, how past experiences shape our thought patterns, and why we can't just turn it off.

We'll talk about what overthinking does to our relationships— how it creates unnecessary tension, builds emotional walls, and keeps us from experiencing real connection. If you've ever pushed someone away because of your own inner dialogue, this section will hit home.

We're not just going to talk about overthinking—we're going to break the cycle.

Throughout this book, you'll find practical, science-backed strategies to calm your mind, retrain your thoughts, and build a more grounded, growth-oriented mindset. These aren't abstract ideas; they're real, actionable techniques that you can start using right away.

You'll learn

- how to recognize overthinking patterns before they take over.
- the difference between healthy reflection and destructive rumination.
- ways to reframe your inner dialogue so it works *for* you, not against you.
- techniques to stop overanalyzing relationships and start living them.
- the secret to balancing logic and intuition in love and connection.
- how to cultivate a calm, clear, and intentional mindset.

This book is about learning to guide your thoughts. Instead of letting your mind spiral into negativity and doubt, you'll develop the ability to pause, reset, and choose thoughts that better serve you and your relationships.

By the time you finish this book, you'll no longer be a prisoner of your own mind. You'll have the tools to stop overthinking, start trusting yourself, and create relationships that feel free, connected, and fulfilling.

I want you to know that I'm not here to sell you the idea that there's a magical switch to turn off overthinking quickly. But I promise you this: If you put these strategies into practice, they will change the way you think, feel, and connect with the people in your life.

So, are you ready to trade overthinking for clarity? To stop questioning every single move and start actually enjoying relationships again?

Then, let's get started.

1

Chapter 1: The Overthinking Trap

At 35, Melissa found herself at a crossroads: two incredible job offers were on the table. One promised financial security and a clear path to leadership, while the other offered creativity and the chance to make a real difference. But instead of excitement, Melissa was consumed by overthinking. She lost sleep replaying every pro and con in her mind, worrying about what others would think, and second-guessing her own abilities. She dissected every possible future, trying to predict which choice would lead to the least regret.

Her anxiety spilled over into her relationship with Jake, her boyfriend of four years. At first, he tried to be supportive—offering reassurance, helping her weigh her options, even making spreadsheets to break things down logically. But Melissa's need for constant validation became exhausting. Every time Jake reassured her, she'd come back with another "what if." She wasn't just overthinking the job offers; she started overanalyzing *everything*—her relationship, their future, whether she was making the right choice by staying with him.

Conversations turned into circular debates. Date nights became brainstorming sessions. And the emotional intimacy they once had started to erode under the weight of her relentless overanalyzing. "Do you even want to be with me?" Jake finally asked one evening, exasperated. That hit her like a punch to the gut. She loved Jake, but her constant need for certainty had pushed him to the edge.

Meanwhile, time kept slipping away. While Melissa agonized over the decision, both job offers were withdrawn, leaving her emptyhanded and defeated. That moment was a wake-up call. Sitting in the wreckage of her overthinking, she realized this wasn't the first time it had cost her something important. She thought about the friendships she had strained by reading too much into texts, the opportunities she had missed by waiting for the "perfect" moment, and the times she had held back in love because she feared making the wrong choice.

It was a painful but transformative moment of clarity: Overthinking wasn't just a habit—it was a pattern that had stolen her joy, confidence, and now, even her relationships. Determined to break free, Melissa began a journey to understand and overcome her overthinking, vowing never to let indecision hold her back again.

If you've ever felt stuck, if any of this sounds remotely familiar, or if your overthinking has created distance in your relationships, I get it. I have shared this space.

The goal of this chapter is to help you recognize the patterns that keep you trapped and, more importantly, show you how to step out of them before they cost you something you can't get back.

What Does Overthinking Look and Feel Like?

Overthinking isn't just the occasional bout of worry or a moment of indecision—it's a full-blown mental marathon that can leave you emotionally drained and physically tense. It's that voice in your head that won't let you rest, replaying conversations, analyzing every possible outcome, and convincing you that you're one misstep away from catastrophe. Sound familiar? Overthinking has a way of hijacking your peace and making even the simplest decisions feel overwhelming. So, how do you know if you're caught in the overthinking trap?

The Endless Loop of Repetitive Thoughts

One of the hallmark signs of overthinking is the mental hamster wheel—the same thoughts circling over and over again without ever landing on a resolution. Maybe you're replaying something you said at dinner last week, convinced you sounded foolish. Or perhaps you're obsessing over an upcoming decision, trying to predict every possible outcome to avoid making a mistake. The irony? Overthinking rarely leads to clarity. Instead, it keeps you stuck, making problems feel bigger than they actually are. Recognizing when your mind is running in circles is the first step toward breaking free. Because let's be real—thinking something *again* for the hundredth time doesn't make it any more useful than the first.

The Physical Toll of Overthinking

Overthinking isn't just a mental game—it takes a serious toll on your body. Racing thoughts often come with physical symptoms: a tight chest, a rapid heartbeat, tense shoulders, or even stomach issues. That's because overthinking is often rooted in anxiety, and your body reacts as if you're in danger, even when you're just lying in bed analyzing a text message. These physical responses are your body's way of signaling that your brain is in overdrive. The good news? Once you recognize these cues, you can start to step in and break the cycle before it spirals.

Self-Criticism: The Hidden Cost of Overthinking

Here's where overthinking really does a number on you—it breeds self-criticism. When you analyze every little thing you say or do, it's easy to start picking yourself apart. *I should have handled that better. Why am I like this? What if they think I'm annoying?* The more you overthink, the harsher that inner critic becomes. Research shows that excessive self-criticism doesn't just mess with your confidence—it triggers stress responses in the body, leading to increased cortisol levels and even impacting your immune system. In other words, overthinking isn't just emotionally exhausting; it's physically harmful, too. Learning to recognize and challenge self-critical thoughts can be a game-changer in breaking free from the overthinking trap.

The Paralysis of Indecision

Overthinkers often struggle with making decisions—whether it's something major, like switching careers, or something minor, like choosing a restaurant. The fear of making the wrong choice leads to decision paralysis, leaving you stuck in a loop of overanalysis and second-guessing. The result? Frustration, missed opportunities, and even a loss of trust in your own instincts. The truth is that no decision comes with a guaranteed outcome, and waiting for certainty is a one-way ticket to inaction. Learning to make quicker, more confident decisions takes practice, but the more you do it, the easier it becomes.

Overthinking feels productive, but in reality, it's a thief of joy, time, and mental energy. The key to overcoming it isn't about silencing your thoughts altogether (that's impossible) but about recognizing when they cross the line from helpful to harmful—and knowing when to let go.

Assessment: Identifying Your Overthinking Patterns

Before we can change something, we have to understand it first. Overthinking isn't random—it has patterns, triggers, and tendencies that show up in predictable ways. The good news? Once you identify your unique overthinking blueprint, you'll have the power to disrupt the cycle before it takes over. This simple worksheet will help you map out your triggers, recognize your tendencies, and create an action plan to start shifting your mindset. Grab a notebook, or better yet, print this out and write your responses down. Let's dive in!

Overthinking Patterns Worksheet

Part 1: Identifying Triggers

First, let's pinpoint the situations that tend to send your thoughts into overdrive. These triggers could be external (like conflict, deadlines, or social interactions) or internal (like self-doubt or past experiences).

-
-
-

Part 2: Recognizing Tendencies

Now that you know your triggers, let's dig into how your mind reacts to them. What are the common thought patterns that show up when overthinking takes hold?

-
-
-

Part 3: Mapping Patterns

This is where we put it all together. By mapping out your triggers and tendencies, you can begin to see the patterns in your overthinking.

-
-
-

Part 4: Taking Action

Awareness is powerful, but taking action is where real change happens. Now, let's create a plan to manage your overthinking when it strikes.

Overthinking can feel automatic, but once you start mapping it out, you'll realize you have more control than you think. The goal isn't to eliminate all thoughts (impossible!) but to recognize when overthinking is no longer helpful and shift gears before it takes over. Keep this worksheet handy, revisit it often, and celebrate every small step you take toward breaking free from the overthinking trap.

Breaking the Overthinking Cycle: Your Action Plan

Now that you've mapped out your overthinking patterns, it's time to do something about them. Overthinking thrives on passivity—the more you sit in it, the stronger it gets. The good news? You can disrupt the cycle. The key is *action*. Below are practical tools to help you recognize when you're overthinking and shift your focus before it spirals out of control.

Journaling: Track Your Triggers

Writing things down is super effective. When your thoughts are tangled up, putting them on paper helps you untangle them. Grab a journal or open a journaling app and try this:

1. Write down what's on your mind, no filter.
2. Identify patterns—do certain situations or people trigger your overthinking?
3. Reflect on what is *actually* happening vs. what your mind is spinning into worst-case scenarios.

Journaling helps you see your thoughts as just that—thoughts, not facts.

Mindfulness Meditation: Train Your Brain to Stay Present

Overthinking drags you into the past or future, but mindfulness keeps you grounded in the present. Here's a simple practice:

1. Close your eyes and focus on your breath.

2. When your mind starts spiraling, acknowledge the thought and gently return to your breath.
3. The more you practice, the easier it becomes to notice overthinking before it takes over.

Mindfulness isn't about clearing your mind. It's about learning to notice your thoughts without getting lost in them.

Cognitive Behavioral Therapy (CBT) Techniques: Reframe the Story

Overthinking often involves distorted thinking—jumping to conclusions, catastrophizing, or assuming the worst. CBT helps you challenge these thoughts:

1. Ask yourself: *Is this thought 100% true, or am I making assumptions?*
2. Replace negative thoughts with balanced, realistic ones.
3. Example: Instead of *I'm going to mess up this presentation,* try *I've prepared, and I'll do my best. That's enough.*

Changing how you talk to yourself changes everything.

Breathing Exercises: Slow Down the Spiral

When your mind races, your body reacts. A simple breathing technique can calm both:

1. Try box breathing: Inhale for 4 seconds, hold for 4, exhale for 4, hold for 4.
2. Repeat until you feel your heart rate slow down.

Your breath is one of the fastest ways to shift your mental state—use it.

Thought-Stopping: Hit the Mental Brakes

Overthinking is like watching a bad movie on repeat. Thought-stopping is your way of hitting the pause button:

1. When you catch yourself spiraling, say "STOP!" (out loud if you need to).
2. Visualize a stop sign, then redirect your focus to something productive.
3. The more you do this, the quicker you'll train your brain to recognize and halt overthinking.

Grounding Techniques: Snap Back to Reality

When you're stuck in your head, your body can pull you back. Try the 5-4-3-2-1 method:

- 5 things you see
- 4 things you can touch
- 3 things you hear
- 2 things you smell
- 1 thing you taste

This interrupts the overthinking cycle and brings you back to the present moment.

Structured Problem-Solving: Take Action Instead of Spinning

Overthinking feels productive, but it's not problem-solving. Instead of ruminating, try this approach:

- Define the issue.
- List possible solutions.
- Choose the most realistic one.
- Take a small action step.

Even tiny actions create momentum—and momentum kills overthinking.

Time Limits: Contain the Overthinking

If your brain insists on analyzing, give it a deadline:

1. Set a 10-minute timer and allow yourself to think about the issue.
2. Once time's up, move on.
3. This tells your brain, *I'll think about this, but I won't let it take over my day.*

There are some variations on this exercise to consider. For example, *I'll allow myself tonight to think about this situation, but tomorrow, I start fresh and let it go.* Or maybe consider, *I am giving myself 24 hours to look at this from all angles, but tomorrow is a new day.*

Physical Activity: Move to Clear Your Mind

Your brain wasn't designed to solve every problem while sitting still. Movement helps:

- Go for a walk.
- Stretch.
- Dance to your favorite song.

Exercise releases stress and helps you reset mentally. Sometimes, the best way to clear your head is to use your body.

Support System: Stop Overthinking Alone

Talking it out can be the quickest way to break the cycle:

- Call a friend and say, "I need to get out of my head. Can you help me gain some perspective?"
- Seek a therapist or coach if overthinking is deeply impacting your life.

You don't have to figure everything out alone. Sometimes, a fresh perspective is all you need.

Breaking the overthinking cycle isn't about never overthinking again—that's impossible. It's about catching yourself sooner and redirecting your energy faster. Each time you interrupt the pattern, you take back control.

Pick one or two tools from this list and start using them today. The more you practice, the easier it gets. You've got this!

Final Thoughts

If you've made it this far, give yourself a moment to appreciate something important—you're starting to notice your over-thinking patterns. And that's a big deal. Awareness is how you start to heal and grow.

We've covered a lot in this chapter. You've learned how overthinking sneaks into your life, keeps you stuck in an endless loop of "what-ifs," and even affects your relationships. You've also taken the first steps in mapping out your triggers and tendencies, and you now have an action plan packed with real, tangible tools to break the cycle. Remember, none of this is about never overthinking again (we're human, not robots). It's about learning to recognize when your thoughts are working for you and when they're working against you. It's about knowing when to step in and shift gears before overthinking hijacks your peace, your decisions, your relationships, and your health.

And speaking of health... overthinking doesn't just feel exhausting—it *is* exhausting. The next chapter dives into exactly why that happens. What's actually going on in your brain when you're stuck in an overthinking spiral? How does it affect your body, your sleep, your mood, and even your immune system? Your brain wasn't designed to operate at full speed 24-7, and when it does, there's a price to pay.

So, take a deep breath. Shake off any lingering tension. And get ready to see overthinking in a whole new way—starting with what it's really doing to your brain and body.

2

Chapter 2: Your Brain on Overthinking

Emma is lying in bed, staring at the ceiling, ruminating about her relationship. Did she come across as needy when she said she hadn't heard from him all day? Should she have waited to text him for the third time? What if he is upset now? What if this damages her relationship?

As her brain spirals into endless "what-ifs," Emma tries to stop the thoughts. But instead of calming down, her mind finds new scenarios to dissect. The more she tries to quiet her brain, the louder it seems to get. Her heart races, her chest feels tight, and sleep becomes a distant dream. By morning, she's exhausted, frustrated, and still no closer to an answer.

This endless loop happens because of how our brains are wired. When Emma starts overthinking, her brain's prefrontal cortex—the part responsible for rational thought— tries to solve the perceived problem.

This cycle not only makes it harder for Emma to think clearly but also prevents her from breaking free. The more her brain tries to fix the problem, the more overwhelmed she feels, leading to mental exhaustion and emotional burnout. Over time, this pattern chips away at her ability to make decisions, relax, and even trust her instincts.

Overthinking isn't just an annoying habit—it's a self-reinforcing loop that hijacks the brain, keeping it stuck in a state of perpetual worry. Breaking free requires recognizing the loop for what it is and finding ways to interrupt it before it spirals out of control.

But here's the good news: just because your brain has learned to overthink doesn't mean it has to stay that way. Understanding the science behind this loop is exactly how you break free.

In this chapter, we'll explore how overthinking rewires the brain, impacts your well-being, and—most importantly—how you can stop the cycle before it takes over. You deserve peace, clarity, and relationships that feel good—without the mental gymnastics.

Let's dive in.

The Neuroscience of Overthinking

If overthinking had a theme song, it would be that annoying tune stuck on repeat in your head—the one you didn't even like in the first place. The more you try to push it out, the louder it gets. And your brain works the same way. Overthinking isn't just something we *do*—it actually changes the way our brain functions, making it harder to think clearly, relax, or trust our instincts. Let's break down what's really happening upstairs when our thoughts go into overdrive.

Brain Activation Patterns: Overthinking Keeps the Alarm System Stuck on High Alert

There you are, about to hit send on a risky text (maybe an "I miss you" to an ex—yikes). Your prefrontal cortex, the rational part of your brain, should be able to evaluate and move on. Instead, your amygdala—the brain's fear center—decides this is a crisis. It sounds the alarm, releasing stress hormones like cortisol, which makes you jittery and anxious.

The problem? The more often you engage in this cycle, the more sensitive your brain becomes to stressors. Over time, your amygdala starts anticipating danger, even when none exists. So now, even the most minor decisions—what to say in a group chat, how your boss phrased their last email—start to feel huge. Your brain literally gets stuck in high alert mode, making it harder to return to a relaxed state. Research shows that chronic overactivation of these stress-response circuits can rewire the brain, making anxiety a default setting.

The Role of Neurotransmitters: A Brain Chemistry Mess

Think of neurotransmitters as your brain's text messages— tiny chemical signals that keep everything running smoothly. Overthinking, however, messes with the delivery system.

For starters, excess cortisol (the stress hormone) doesn't just make you anxious—it also disrupts serotonin, the neurotransmitter responsible for happiness and emotional balance. This is why overthinking can lead to full-blown mood issues like anxiety and depression. And dopamine, the neurotransmitter tied to motivation and pleasure, also takes a hit, which explains why overthinkers often feel drained, indecisive, and emotionally exhausted (*Serotonin*, 2022).

Imagine spending hours agonizing over a tough conversation with your partner. By the time you actually have the talk, you're too stressed to think straight, and instead of feeling relieved, you feel even worse. That's what happens when overthinking messes with your brain chemistry—it hijacks your ability to process emotions effectively.

Cognitive Function Decline: When Your Brain Feels Like a Browser With 50 Tabs Open

How many times have you walked into a room and immediately forgotten why you were there? That's your brain on overthinking. Constant rumination takes up so much mental bandwidth that it affects your ability to concentrate, retain memories, and make decisions.

Think of it this way: Your brain is like a computer. Overthinking is the equivalent of running too many programs at once— everything slows down, glitches happen, and the whole system gets overwhelmed. Studies show that excessive worrying impairs working memory, making it harder to retain information

(Meek, 2024). It also reduces problem-solving abilities because your brain is too busy running worst-case scenarios to focus on solutions.

For example, let's say you're stuck on a work email, rewriting it for the tenth time because you're convinced it has to be perfect. But the more you tweak it, the harder it becomes to even think clearly. That's because overthinking drains your cognitive energy, leaving you mentally paralyzed. The cycle continues: The more exhausted your brain feels, the more mistakes you make, leading to—you guessed it—more overthinking.

The Plastic Brain: You Can Rewire This Mess

Your brain isn't doomed to overthink forever. Thanks to neuroplasticity—your brain's ability to rewire and form new connections—you can break free from this pattern (Cherry, 2024).

Think of your thoughts as hiking trails. The more you travel the overthinking path, the more defined it becomes. But if you actively choose a different path—like reframing negative thoughts, focusing on mindfulness, or interrupting rumination—you start to form new neural pathways. Over time, this makes healthy thinking patterns easier and overthinking less automatic.

For instance, imagine you catch yourself spiraling over something your partner said and how you responded. Instead of replaying every possible reaction, you pause and say, "I've done my part. I can't control their reaction." That simple shift disrupts the overthinking loop and signals your brain to form a different response pattern.

Through practices like mindfulness, cognitive restructuring, and even physical movement (we will get into these soon), you can teach your brain to stop treating everyday worries like emergencies. The more you reinforce these new patterns, the easier it becomes to trust yourself, make decisions, and, most importantly, breathe.

Overthinking Is Reversible—If You Catch It

Your brain wasn't built to run in stress mode 24-7. Overthinking might feel automatic, but it's just a habit your brain has learned—and habits can be unlearned. When you begin to understand how overthinking alters brain function, you can start taking steps to break the cycle, calm your nervous system, and reclaim mental clarity.

Because at the end of the day, your brain doesn't need more overanalyzing. It needs peace. And that's something you can create.

Analysis Paralysis Explained: Why Decision-Making Feels Impossible

Have you ever stood in the toothpaste aisle, staring at 47 different kinds of toothpaste, completely unable to pick one? Whitening, extra whitening, cavity protection, enamel repair, charcoal-infused, baking soda... suddenly, you're questioning every dental decision you've ever made. That, my friend, is analysis paralysis in action.

Now, take that same feeling and apply it to bigger decisions— relationships, careers, finances, life choices—and you've got a full-blown mental traffic jam. Analysis paralysis happens when we get so caught up in trying to make the perfect decision that we end up making no decision at all. Let's break down why this happens and, more importantly, how to escape it.

Overwhelmed by Options: Too Many Choices, Too Much Pressure

How often have you spent so much time debating where to eat that by the time you decide, you're no longer hungry? That's because when we have too many choices, our brain struggles to weigh all the factors, fearing we'll make the wrong choice. Instead of picking something and moving on, we stall, hoping the right or perfect answer will magically reveal itself. That is an impossible dream.

If you find yourself endlessly comparing job offers, debating whether to text someone back, or staring at a menu for an absurd amount of time, you might be stuck in analysis paralysis.

Obsessive Information Gathering: Researching Yourself Into Exhaustion

Analysis paralysis often disguises itself as being responsible. You tell yourself, *I just need to gather more information,* so you research, ask for opinions, watch YouTube reviews, and poll everyone you know. But instead of helping, this flood of information only makes the decision feel harder.

For example, you need to buy a new laptop. Instead of picking one based on your needs, you deep-dive into specs, read 100+ reviews, watch comparison videos, and ask multiple people for their opinions. Two weeks later, you still haven't made a purchase because what if there's a better one? Don't even get me started on how this same scenario plays out in dating apps!

When information-gathering shifts from helpful research to avoidance, that's a red flag.

Stuck in a Loop of "What-Ifs"

One of the biggest traps of analysis paralysis is the endless cycle of "what if."

- *What if I make the wrong decision?*
- *What if I regret it later?*

27

· *What if there's a better option I haven't considered yet?*

These thoughts keep you stuck in decision limbo, convinced that if you just think hard enough, you'll somehow predict the future. (You won't.) Instead of making progress, you stay trapped in an exhausting loop of self-doubt.

How to Overcome Analysis Paralysis

You now know what analysis paralysis is and how to identify it. Great! But, well... how do you make it all stop? Great question. Let's break that down:

Set a Decision Deadline

Give yourself a time limit. Period. Instead of waiting for the "perfect" answer to magically appear, decide that you'll make a choice by a specific deadline.

For example, if you're agonizing over booking a vacation, tell yourself, *By 5 p.m. today, I will pick a destination and book the flight. No more second-guessing.* This forces you to take action instead of endlessly debating.

Limit Your Options

Too many choices lead to overwhelm. Instead of trying to consider every possibility, narrow it down to two or three options. Ask yourself:

- *Which option best aligns with my values or goals?*
- *Which one excites me the most?*
- *Which one would I choose if I had to decide right now?*

For example, if you're stuck choosing between five job offers, eliminate the ones that don't excite you or don't align with your long-term goals. Now, instead of five options, you only have two. Decision-making just got way easier.

Trust Your Intuition and Take Action

At some point, you have to stop thinking and just do it. No decision is ever 100% perfect. The goal isn't to guarantee a flawless outcome—it's to move forward and adjust as needed. Trust that you're capable of handling whatever comes next.

For example, if you've been debating whether to ask that person out but keep hesitating because what if they're not into you? Instead of overthinking, just ask. Taking action, even if it doesn't go your way, creates momentum—and momentum leads to clarity.

Action Beats Overthinking Every Time

The more you train yourself to act rather than overanalyze, the easier decision-making becomes. Remember, no single choice will make or break your life. If you make a decision and it doesn't work out? You learn, pivot, and move forward. The real mistake is staying stuck.

So, go ahead—make that call, send that text, book that trip. Your brain will thank you.

Social Media's Role in Overthinking: The Perfect Storm for a Busy Brain

In today's world, most of us don't just use social media, we live on it. It's the first thing we check in the morning, the last thing we scroll at night, and our go-to when we're bored, anxious, or avoiding something (like making an actual decision). But while social media can be entertaining, it also has a sneaky way of feeding our worst overthinking tendencies.

From endless information overload to the pressure of looking like we have it all figured out, social media doesn't just distract us—it rewires our brains to overanalyze everything. Here's how.

Information Overload: Too Much Input, Not Enough Clarity

How many times have you been down a social media rabbit hole only to emerge two hours later, overwhelmed and more confused than when you started? That's the curse of too much information.

Social media bombards us with an endless stream of opinions, news, trends, and unsolicited advice. One minute, you're looking at a post about mindful living, and the next, you're drowning in conflicting views on nutrition, relationship advice, and 20 different "Here's how to find the person of your dreams" posts. It's like trying to drink from a fire hose—your brain just can't process it all.

Instead of finding clarity, this flood of information creates decision fatigue. The more options, advice, and perspectives you absorb, the harder it becomes to separate useful information from noise. You end up second-guessing yourself, postponing decisions, and stuck in analysis paralysis (yep, we're back to that).

The result? More rumination, more self-doubt, and a brain that never really turns off.

Comparison Culture: The Fastest Way to Feel Like You're Not Enough

We've all seen those "perfect" vacation, relationship, or career update posts and immediately started questioning our own life. That's the comparison trap, and social media is its breeding ground.

This is when we have to remember that social media isn't real life—it's a highlight reel. Do you remember when our parents taught us about "pretend" and "make-believe"? Yep, same thing. People post the best angles, the happiest moments, the filtered versions of their reality. You are not going to see the screaming toddlers, the messy kitchens, the burnt dinners, or the husband sleeping on the couch after a fight. And yet, our brains compare those polished snapshots to our messy, unfiltered real lives. The result?

- *Why don't I have my dream job yet?*
- *Should I be traveling more?*
- *Why does their relationship seem so effortless?*

Social media fuels insecurity by making us feel like we're constantly behind—like we're missing out, not doing enough, or somehow failing. And when we internalize these doubts, we start overanalyzing everything—our choices, our achievements, our self-worth. It's a never-ending loop of "Am I enough?" that keeps our minds spinning.

Social Validation Seeking: The Double-Edged Sword of Likes and Comments

Let's talk about that tiny dopamine hit we get when someone likes our post. Or even better, leaves a comment like, "Wow, you look amazing!" or "Do you ever age???" Feels good, right? But the more we tie our self-worth to external validation, the worse our overthinking gets.

Are you guilty of posting something and then checking your phone to see if people reacted? Or deleted a post because it didn't "perform" well? That's social validation seeking in action.

Social media creates an environment where we're constantly waiting for feedback—on our photos, our opinions, our experiences. And when we don't get the response we hoped for, we start second-guessing ourselves:

- *Was that too much?*
- *Should I have worded that differently?*
- *Do people even notice I am here?*

This obsessive monitoring of engagement fuels anxiety and reinforces the habit of overthinking every interaction. Instead of expressing ourselves freely, we start filtering our thoughts, curating our image, and overanalyzing how we appear rather than how we feel.

Escapism vs. Engagement: The Social Media Tug-of-War

Sometimes, social media feels like a break from overthinking. Scrolling through memes, watching funny videos, or losing yourself in a TikTok rabbit hole can feel like a temporary escape. But social media often increases anxiety in the long run.

While it may provide a short-term distraction, excessive social media use

- reduces the time available for real-life interactions, making us feel more disconnected.
- reinforces dependency, so we turn to scrolling instead of actually solving our problems.
- keeps our brains in constant input mode, making it harder

to process emotions and thoughts effectively.

Instead of genuinely engaging with our lives—talking to people, making decisions, taking action—we get stuck observing other people's curated lives, overanalyzing our own, and feeling increasingly dissatisfied.

Breaking Free: Using Social Media Without Letting It Use You

Social media isn't inherently bad, but how we engage with it matters. If you find that scrolling leaves you anxious, drained, or stuck in overthinking loops, try this:

- **Set boundaries:** Limit the time you spend scrolling, especially before bed (overthinking plus blue light equals disaster).
- **Curate your feed:** Unfollow accounts that make you feel inadequate. Follow people who inspire, educate, or actually make you feel good.
- **Post for you, not for validation:** If you like something, share it. Don't obsess over numbers—your worth isn't measured in likes.
- **Prioritize real life:** If social media is replacing real conversations, interactions, and decisions, it's time to step back. The best moments in life don't need an audience.

Social media can be a tool or a trap—it depends on how you use it. If you find yourself overthinking more because of what you see online, take a step back. The goal isn't to disconnect from the world—it's to reconnect with yourself.

Because at the end of the day, no algorithm, comment, or curated post should have the power to dictate your happiness. You're in control—always.

Action Plan: Breaking Neural Loops to Rewire Overthinking Patterns

We now know that our brain is changeable, thanks to neuro-plasticity, which means that with the right strategies, you can literally rewire your thought patterns. Remember, the key is to disrupt the overthinking loop before it spirals out of control. Here's your step-by-step action plan to break free.

Step 1: Focus on Awareness and Acknowledgment

Before you can stop overthinking, you need to recognize when it's happening. That's where awareness comes in.

- **Track your thoughts:** Keep a thought journal to notice when and where overthinking shows up. Write down recurring worries, triggers, and patterns. You might start to notice that certain times of the day (hello, 2 a.m.), certain topics (relationships, work, self-doubt), or specific situations send your brain into overdrive.
- **Ask yourself:** *Is this problem real, or am I just imagining worst-case scenarios?* Often, overthinking is just your brain inventing problems that don't exist.

Step 2: Use Mindfulness Practices

Mindfulness is like the off switch for overthinking. It helps your brain focus on right *now* instead of running a mental marathon into the future.

- **Try a daily mindfulness meditation (10–15 minutes):** No, you don't have to become a monk. Just sitting quietly and observing your thoughts without engaging with them can train your brain to slow down.
- **Use mindful breathing techniques:** The next time you catch yourself spiraling, try this: inhale for four counts, hold for four, exhale for four. Repeat. It helps break the mental loop and calm your nervous system.

Step 3: Incorporate Physical Movement

You can't overthink and be fully present in movement at the same time. Exercise forces your brain to shift gears, flooding it with feel-good chemicals instead of stress hormones.

- **Move your body regularly (30 minutes, 3–5 times a week):** Whether it's walking, running, or dancing in your living room, movement disrupts overthinking patterns.
- **Try yoga or Pilates:** These combine physical movement and mindfulness, making them perfect for calming a busy brain.

Step 4: Try Cognitive Restructuring

Overthinking thrives on unchecked, exaggerated fears. Time to cross-examine those thoughts.

- **Use cognitive behavioral techniques:** When a negative thought pops up, ask:
- *Is this true? (Where's the evidence?)*
- *Am I catastrophizing? (Am I making this bigger than it is?)*
- *What's a more balanced way to look at this?*
- **Replace negative thoughts with affirmations:** If your brain says, *I always mess things up,* reframe it to, *I've handled challenges before, and I'll handle this, too.*

Step 5: Set Thought Boundaries

Your brain will always find something to worry about. Instead of fighting it, contain it.

- **Designate specific "worry times" (10–15 minutes per day):** When anxious thoughts show up, tell yourself, *Not now. I'll think about this at 5 p.m.* This reduces the urge to ruminate all day.
- **Use timers:** Give yourself 5–10 minutes to think something through, then move on. The goal isn't not thinking—it's productive thinking.

Step 6: Utilize Mental Distraction Techniques

Your brain needs something better to do than overanalyze every life decision. Redirect your thoughts into active engagement.

- **Get creative:** Paint, journal, cook, knit—anything that engages your hands and brain. Creativity is a natural antidote to overthinking.
- **Use puzzles or brain games:** Sudoku, crosswords, or even a good book can pull your mind out of rumination mode.

Step 7: Find Social Connection

Isolation is an overthinker's worst enemy. Connection helps put things into perspective.

- **Talk to someone:** A trusted friend, partner, or family member can help you see things more clearly.
- **Join group activities or community events:** Engaging in hobbies, volunteering, or social groups reminds you there's more to life than the inside of your head.

Step 8: Make Healthy Lifestyle Choices

Your brain is a physical organ—it needs the right fuel to function properly.

- **Eat brain-boosting foods:** Omega-3s (found in fish, wal-

nuts, and flaxseeds) support cognitive function. Limit caffeine and sugar, which can spike anxiety.
· **Prioritize sleep (7–9 hours per night):** Lack of sleep fuels overthinking. A well-rested brain is less likely to spiral.

Step 9: Limit Information Overload

Your brain is already overanalyzing—don't add to the chaos.

· **Reduce negative news and social media exposure:** Too much information tricks your brain into believing you need to process it all. You don't.
· **Set screen time limits:** Check social media and news intentionally, not impulsively. Instead of constant scrolling, choose a few key times per day.

Step 10: Seek Professional Help

Sometimes, overthinking is tied to deeper anxiety, trauma, or perfectionism. Therapy can provide customized strategies for managing it.

· **Consider counseling or coaching:** A therapist can help you untangle thought patterns that keep you stuck.
· **Explore support groups:** Connecting with others who experience similar struggles can help reduce feelings of isolation and normalize the experience of overthinking.

Step 11: Evaluate and Adjust

This process is unique to you. What works for someone else may not be *your* solution, so experiment and refine.

- **Review your progress weekly or monthly:** What's helping? What's not? Adjust accordingly.
- **Celebrate small wins:** Every time you successfully interrupt an overthinking spiral, you're rewiring your brain. Acknowledge that progress.

With practice, your brain will learn new, healthier patterns. You'll spend less time stuck in analysis and more time living your life. And that is the real win.

Final Thoughts

If you've made it this far, you're already on your way to breaking free from the overthinking loop—and that's huge. You've uncovered how your brain gets stuck in overanalysis, how social media fuels the spiral, and most importantly, how to rewire your mind to think in healthier, more productive ways.

Now, overthinking isn't going to disappear overnight. But every time you recognize it, challenge it, and redirect it, you're teaching your brain a new way of operating. And with time, this new way becomes your default.

Think of it like training a dog. At first, your brain (like an excitable puppy) wants to run off in every direction—chasing every worry, dissecting every conversation, and second-guessing every decision. But with patience and consistency, you can train it to sit, stay, and actually relax.

And that's exactly where we're heading next.

In the next chapter, we're diving into practical, science-backed strategies to help you quiet the mental noise, relax your nervous system, and create the kind of inner peace that no amount of social media scrolling or late-night overanalyzing can shake.

So, take a deep breath. You've done the hard work of understanding the problem. Now, let's step into the solution to gain a calm mind.

3

Chapter 3: Calming the Mind

Jeremy had been married for 10 years, and those years were filled with love, laughter —and, if he was being honest—some epic arguments. Most of those fights? They weren't about what his wife said but what his mind twisted it into.

Take the time she bought him new pants. Sweet gesture, right? Not to Jeremy's overthinking brain. *Does she think I've gained weight?* he'd spiraled. The thought festered for days, growing bigger with each passing moment, until he finally erupted with, "Why didn't you just say I need to lose weight instead of buying me pants?" The hurt in her eyes still haunted him.

Then there was the restaurant incident. She suggested trying a new place downtown, and Jeremy was sure it meant she was bored—bored with the food, bored with their routine, bored with him. That thought tumbled into more assumptions. Before dessert even arrived, they were in a full-blown argument about her "being unhappy."

When his marriage ended, Jeremy realized just how much his overthinking had sabotaged their connection. He vowed to do better in his next relationship. But now, two years into dating someone new, he could see the same patterns creeping in.

Last week, his girlfriend said, "Let's book a weekend getaway." It sounded innocent enough, but his mind ran wild. *Does she think I'm not fun anymore? Am I not putting in enough effort? Does she want to get away from me?* He could feel the spiral begin: the racing thoughts, the tight chest, the urge to unleash the storm building inside.

But this time, Jeremy did something different. Instead of reacting, he grabbed his hiking boots and headed for his favorite trail.

Out in the fresh air, surrounded by towering trees and the rhythmic crunch of his boots on the dirt path, Jeremy felt his mind begin to slow. The rush of the stream nearby drowned out his anxious thoughts, and the scent of pine seemed to clear his mental fog.

He stopped at a scenic overlook, taking in the sprawling view, and asked himself the question that had become his lifeline: *Is this from my past or my present?* When he thought about it, he realized his girlfriend had given no indication that she was dissatisfied or bored. The fear he felt wasn't about her—it was a shadow from his marriage, from all the times he hadn't felt good enough.

"Okay," he said out loud, letting the word echo into the valley below. "This is from my past. Not my present." By the time Jeremy got back to his car, he felt grounded again. He reframed the situation, recognizing her suggestion as a thoughtful way to spend more quality time together. Instead of diving into an argument, he called her and said, "That getaway sounds amazing. Let's start planning it."

It wasn't easy, and it wasn't perfect, but it was progress. Jeremy had learned that calming his mind wasn't about ignoring his thoughts but giving them a chance to breathe and then deciding whether they deserved his energy.

For him, hiking wasn't just exercise; it was a way to walk his way out of his own head. Out there, surrounded by nature, he found the clarity he needed to stop the overthinking spiral before it could wreak havoc on his relationship.

Because now, Jeremy understood: Sometimes, the best way to move forward is to take a step back—and maybe a few steps up a mountain trail.

When your mind calms down, everything else starts to fall into place. Relationships feel easier, communication flows naturally, and you can enjoy moments instead of being trapped in your head.

Throughout this chapter, we'll explore practical strategies that helped Jeremy—and can help you—calm the mental noise. We'll cover simple techniques like grounding exercises, breathwork, and mindfulness practices tailored specifically for overthinkers. These aren't complicated rituals that require hours of your day. They're small, manageable tools you can use when your thoughts start to spiral.

Think of a calm mind as the foundation for healthier, happier relationships—starting with the one you have with yourself.

What a Calm Mind Feels Like

I want you to envision yourself sitting by a still lake at dawn. The surface is glassy, perfectly reflecting the sky above, undisturbed by ripples or waves. Inhale. What do you smell? Listen. What do you hear? Pay attention to the tension in your body. Is there any?

This is what a calm mind feels like. Thoughts exist, but they settle instead of spinning wildly. There's clarity, space, and a kind of inner stillness that allows you to reflect without judgment or panic. It's the difference between watching leaves float by on that same water versus standing in a storm where waves are crashing at you at once.

When your mind is calm, you're no longer in survival mode. You're not overanalyzing every scenario or decision. Instead, you're present, grounded, and able to enjoy the moment without feeling like your brain is running a marathon.

So, how do you know when you've tapped into that calm? It often starts with physical cues:

· **Relaxed shoulders:** No more wearing them as earrings.

45

- **Slowed breathing:** Deeper inhales and longer exhales that don't feel forced.
- **Softened chest:** That tight, anxious grip around your heart releases.

Emotionally, you notice there's less urgency. You feel less compelled to react instantly and more able to respond thoughtfully. Conversations no longer feel like a battlefield where you have to say the right thing or defend yourself. There's space—a pause between a thought and your reaction—giving you the power to choose your response.

The Contrast: Overthinking vs. Calm

Now, let's talk about overthinking. It can feel like standing in the middle of Times Square during rush hour, with a million blinking lights and honking horns all demanding your attention. Your heart races, your breathing gets shallow, and your mind runs like a hamster on a wheel, going nowhere fast.

It's exhausting. And it's no wonder it spills into your relationships, making simple interactions feel overwhelming or tense.

In contrast, a calm mind is like stepping out of that chaos and into a peaceful room where everything has its place. Imagine sitting at a clean, clutter-free desk. You can focus on the task at hand without sifting through piles of papers or random junk. Your mind feels spacious, organized, and most importantly, manageable.

Take Ashley, for example. She used to overthink every word said to her new partner. *Was that too blunt? Should I have added an emoji? What if they think I'm mad?* Her mind would spiral, leading to unnecessary arguments based on assumptions rather than facts. After practicing mindfulness and learning to calm her thoughts, Ashley noticed a shift. She found herself pausing before responding, breathing through moments of anxiety, and approaching conversations with clarity rather than panic. Her relationship improved—not because her partner changed, but because her mind did.

Achieving a calm mind isn't about eliminating thoughts—it's about organizing them. It's about creating space so that your thoughts don't overpower you. And in relationships, that calmness allows you to truly connect, listen, and respond from a place of understanding rather than fear or anxiety.

The goal? To swap the chaotic buzzing of overthinking for the stillness of that peaceful lake—because that's where clarity, connection, and peace live.

The Science of a Calm Mind

We've all heard how important it is to stay calm, but have you ever wondered why calmness feels so good—not just emotionally, but physically, too?

47

Neuroscience of Calmness: Your Brain's Rest and Digest Mode

When your mind is calm, it's not just about feeling good—there's actual brain chemistry at play. The star of the show? Your parasympathetic nervous system—also known as your body's rest-and-digest mode. This system steps in to slow everything down, helping you relax after stress spikes. It's the counterbalance to the fight or flight response.

When the parasympathetic system is activated (Tindle & Tadi, 2022)

- your cortisol levels (the stress hormone) drop.
- your heart rate slows down.
- breathing deepens naturally.
- your body starts focusing on maintenance tasks like digestion and repair.

Fun fact: Studies show that mindfulness practices like deep breathing can reduce cortisol levels by up to 20% in just a few weeks (Ezzat Obaya et al., 2023). That's huge for your mental clarity and overall health.

Think of it like this. When you're calm, your brain isn't burning through fuel on stress. Instead, it's focusing on keeping things running smoothly, helping you think clearer and feel better.

Impact on Emotional Regulation: The Prefrontal Cortex vs. The Amygdala

Ever snapped at someone and instantly regretted it? Yeah, you can thank your amygdala for that—your brain's emotional reaction center. It's the part of your brain that sounds the alarm when you feel threatened, stressed, or emotional. But the amygdala isn't always great at discerning real danger from minor frustrations, like a passive-aggressive text or a rude comment.

When you're stressed or overthinking, the amygdala takes control, leading to knee-jerk reactions. But when your mind is calm? That's when the prefrontal cortex—the rational, decision-making part of your brain—gets to take the wheel.

This shift allows you to

- think before reacting.
- respond thoughtfully instead of emotionally.
- navigate conflicts with more patience and clarity.

A Harvard study found that regular mindfulness meditation actually shrinks the amygdala over time while strengthening the prefrontal cortex (Powell, 2018). Translation? You become less reactive and more in control during emotional moments.

Calmness and Relationships: How a Steady Mind Improves Communication

We've all been in those conversations that start small and suddenly spiral into full-blown arguments. Often, that's the result of stress or overthinking ramping up emotional responses. But when your mind is calm, you can approach disagreements differently.

Research found that couples who practiced stress-reducing techniques (like breathing exercises or mindfulness) before difficult conversations were 40% less likely to escalate into arguments. They also reported higher levels of satisfaction and connection in their relationships (Wilson et al., 2024).

When you're calm, you

- listen more actively instead of planning your next come-back.
- are less defensive and more open to others' perspectives.
- handle disagreements without turning them into emotional battlegrounds.

Take Mark and Lisa, for example. Mark used to get defensive anytime Lisa brought up issues in their relationship. His stress response would kick in, leading to reactive comments like, "Why are you always criticizing me?"

After starting a mindfulness practice (just 10 minutes of deep breathing daily), Mark noticed he was less triggered during these talks. He could pause, breathe, and actually hear what Lisa was saying without feeling personally attacked. Over time, their communication improved—and their relationship grew stronger.

Mind-Body Connection: When the Mind Calms, the Body Follows

Here's where it all comes full circle. A calm mind doesn't just make you feel emotionally better—it impacts your entire body.

When stress levels drop

- blood pressure lowers—reducing strain on your heart.
- digestion improves—since your body is no longer in "survival mode."
- the immune system strengthens—because it's not constantly battling stress hormones.

A study by Johns Hopkins University found that mindfulness-based stress reduction programs significantly lowered blood pressure and reduced anxiety in participants over an eight-week period (*Mindfulness Meditation*, n.d.).

Think of your mind and body like roommates—when one is messy and chaotic, the other feels the impact. But when the mind clears, the body breathes a sigh of relief, too.

A calm mind isn't just a luxury—it's a powerful tool that positively impacts every part of your life, from how you feel physically to how you communicate in your relationships. Science backs this up: Lowering stress, improving emotional regulation, and strengthening your mind-body connection can transform not just how you think but how you live and love.

And the best part? You don't need hours of meditation or expensive programs. Even a few minutes of mindful breathing each day can activate your rest and digest mode, helping you shift from chaos to calm—and creating better, healthier connections along the way.

Overthinking Easers: Practical Tools to Clear the Mental Clutter

In all honesty, overthinking is like having a song stuck in your head, except it's your own anxious thoughts playing on repeat. But you can hit pause. Learning to recognize when your brain starts spinning and giving yourself space to reset can change everything. It's like stepping off the hamster wheel and realizing, *Hey, I actually have control over this!*

Here are some practical, easy-to-try tools to help ease over-thinking and bring in that sweet, sweet mental clarity.

Meditation: Training Your Brain to Stay Present

I know, I know—meditation sounds like one of those things people say you should do, but you're not exactly sure where to start. The good news? Meditation doesn't have to mean sitting cross-legged chanting "om." It's simply about training your brain to focus on the now instead of replaying that awkward thing you said in 2013..

Where can you start?

- **Breath awareness:** Sit comfortably, close your eyes (or not, no pressure), and focus on your breath. Inhale... count to four. Exhale... count to four. That's it. When your mind wanders, gently bring it back to your breath.
- **Guided meditations:** If sitting in silence isn't your jam, apps like Headspace or Calm offer guided meditations that walk you through it step by step. Even 5–10 minutes can make a huge difference.

Meditation activates your brain's prefrontal cortex (hello, rational thinking!) and helps calm the overactive amygdala (the drama queen responsible for emotional overreactions). Over time, this makes it easier to catch yourself when overthinking kicks in and gently shift gears.

Journaling: Getting Thoughts Out of Your Head and Onto Paper

Not everyone loves journaling—and that's okay. But hear me out. Overthinking thrives when thoughts stay trapped in your mind, swirling like a tornado. Journaling acts like an emotional drain, letting all that mental gunk flow out onto paper.

Here's how to make it work for you:

- **Brain dumping:** Open a notebook and write whatever pops into your head. No structure, no filters. Just let it all spill out.
- **Thought snapshots:** If you're not into long entries, try bullet points. Jot down quick thoughts, worries, or even wins from the day.
- **The *What's bothering me?* prompt:** Ask yourself this simple question and write down whatever comes up. It's amazing how often the real issue surfaces.

Take Jane. She was caught in a loop of overanalyzing every interaction at work, convinced her boss secretly hated her. One day, she tried journaling out her thoughts. Turns out, the root of her worry wasn't her boss—it was her fear of failure. Writing it out helped her see the bigger picture and stop fixating on every email and meeting.

Mindfulness Practices: Finding Calm in Everyday Moments

Mindfulness is just a fancy word for paying attention to now—without judgment. It's about bringing your focus back to the present, which naturally quiets that overthinking brain.

Here are some easy mindfulness practices to try:

- **Mindful eating:** Next time you eat, really taste your food. Notice the textures, flavors, and smells. It sounds simple, but focusing fully on the act of eating pulls you into the moment.
- **Mindful walking:** Whether you're strolling through your neighborhood or the park, notice how your feet hit the

ground, the sound of birds, or even the way the wind feels on your face.
· **Mindful pauses in conversations:** During a heated argument or tense moment, take a conscious breath before responding. It gives your brain that crucial pause to respond thoughtfully instead of reacting impulsively.

Remember, mindfulness activates the parasympathetic nervous system, calming both your mind and body. Plus, it teaches you to observe your thoughts without getting swept away by them.

Nature Therapy: Using the Outdoors to Reset Your Mind

There's a reason people say "Get some fresh air" when you're stressed—it works. Nature has a calming effect on the brain, helping to reduce overthinking and boost mental clarity.

A Stanford study found that walking in nature reduces rumination (aka repetitive negative thinking) and lowers activity in the part of the brain linked to overthinking (Jordan, 2015).

Jason, a self-proclaimed overthinker, used to spiral after work—replaying conversations and stressing about deadlines. Then, he started taking short evening walks in the nearby park. No music, no podcasts—just him and the trees. Within days, he noticed a shift. His mind felt clearer, less cluttered, and he slept better.

Pro tip: You don't need a forest—any outdoor space will do.

Even a walk around the block or sitting in the grass of your own backyard can help.

The Five-Minute Rule: Making It Easier to Start

Here's the thing: Committing to long mindfulness sessions or deep journaling can feel overwhelming, especially when your brain's already in overdrive. That's where the five-minute rule comes in.

Here's how it works:

- Tell yourself you only need to do the activity (meditation, journaling, walking, etc.) for five minutes.
- No pressure to go longer—but if you do? Great!
- It's all about starting small and lowering the barrier to entry.

Often, starting is the hardest part. But once you're in it, you'll likely keep going. Even if you only do five minutes, that's still five minutes of calm you didn't have before.

Overthinking can feel like being stuck in a mental traffic jam— horns blaring, thoughts piling up, and no clear path forward. But these tools? They're like building an off-ramp to peace.

The key is recognizing when your brain starts spiraling and pausing long enough to say, "I don't have to follow this thought all the way down the rabbit hole." Whether it's a five-minute breathing exercise, a quick journaling session, or a walk around the block, you have the power to shift from chaos to clarity—one small step at a time.

The Health Benefits of a Calm Mind

We've all been there—lying in bed, staring at the ceiling, your brain doing its best impression of a runaway train. You're replaying that awkward thing you said five years ago or spiraling through tomorrow's to-do list. Overthinking has this sneaky way of creeping into every corner of our lives—our sleep, our work, our health, and especially our relationships.

But calming your mind isn't just about feeling better emotionally—it has real, life-changing benefits. When you recognize how overthinking impacts your life and relationships, leaning into the perks of a calm mind becomes a total game-changer. Let's break it down.

Improved Sleep: Goodbye Racing Thoughts, Hello Zzz's

Overthinking and sleep are mortal enemies. Ever crawled into bed *exhausted* but suddenly wide awake because your brain decides it's the perfect time to replay every embarrassing moment from high school? Yeah, same.

A calm mind flips that script. Without racing thoughts hijacking bedtime, it's easier to fall asleep—and stay asleep. A study found that mindfulness practices significantly reduced insomnia symptoms and helped participants fall asleep faster

(Jermann et al., 2024).

Anna, a chronic overthinker, used to lie awake for hours replaying conversations from her day. Then, she started a simple evening mindfulness routine—just five minutes of breathwork before bed. Within a week, she noticed she was falling asleep quicker and waking up less during the night.

When your mind is calm, sleep comes easier, and quality sleep means better mood, sharper focus, and—let's be honest—less coffee dependency.

Enhanced Focus: Less Mental Chatter, More Clarity

Overthinking is overwhelming and makes focusing on one thing nearly impossible. But when your mind is calm? You can focus on just the task at hand.

Why does it matter?

- You're more productive (hello, shorter workdays!).
- You're more present in conversations—actually listening instead of planning your grocery list mid-chat.
- You make decisions faster and with more confidence.

Think about the last time you tried to read a book or write an email but kept checking your phone or overanalyzing a conversation. Now, imagine doing the same task with a clear, focused mind—no distractions, no spirals. That's the power of calm.

Boosted Resilience: Bouncing Back Like a Pro

It's no secret that life is messy and chaotic. But how you react to them often depends on your mental state. An overthinking mind tends to catastrophize, making minor issues feel like massive disasters. A calm mind, on the other hand, helps you handle challenges with grace and resilience.

Here's how:

- You're less reactive and more reflective.
- You can see the bigger picture instead of getting caught up in minor details.
- You bounce back quicker from setbacks because you're not stuck in a spiral of "what ifs."

A study found that individuals who practiced mindfulness were better at regulating emotions during stressful events, leading to increased resilience (Oh et al., 2022).

Take Kevin. He used to spiral into anxiety any time he made a mistake at work, convinced he was about to be fired. After practicing mindfulness and calming techniques, he noticed a shift. When a project went sideways, instead of panicking, he took a breath, assessed the situation, and problem-solved. The result? Less stress, better solutions, and way fewer late-night panic spirals.

Physical Health Perks: A Calm Mind = A Happier Body

Your mind and body are like that couple who finish each other's sentences—they're deeply connected. When your brain is constantly overthinking, your body reacts with stress responses: elevated cortisol, increased heart rate, shallow breathing, and muscle tension.

But when you calm your mind? Your body follows suit.

The physical benefits of a calm mind include (Powell, 2018):

- **Lower blood pressure:** Chronic stress is a major contributor to hypertension.
- **Improved digestion:** Ever had "nervous stomach" before a big presentation? A calm mind helps your digestive system function properly.
- **Stronger immune system:** Less stress means your body can focus on fighting germs, not perceived threats.
- **More energy:** Constant overthinking is exhausting. A calm mind gives you that "I got a full night's sleep" kind of energy.

A study found that mindfulness practices reduced inflammation markers in the body, improving overall health and lowering the risk of chronic diseases (Black & Slavich, 2016).

Stronger Relationships: More Patience, Empathy, and Connection

Let's be honest—overthinking can wreak havoc on relationships. You might overanalyze texts (*Why did they use a period instead of a smiley face?*), misinterpret comments, or jump to worst-case scenarios. It creates unnecessary tension and can make communication harder than it needs to be.

A calm mind changes that.

Here's how:

- **Patience:** You're less reactive and more willing to listen before jumping to conclusions.
- **Empathy:** A calm mind creates space to see others' perspectives, not just your own.
- **Clear communication:** You're better at expressing your thoughts without them being clouded by assumptions or emotions.

When your mind is calm, your relationships thrive. You're able to show up as your best self—empathetic, patient, and fully present.

The Big Picture: Why It Matters

Overthinking might feel like a personal quirk, but its impact is wide-reaching—from your health to your relationships. But calming your mind isn't just about stopping the negative; it's about unlocking all the positives.

With a calm mind, you

- sleep better.
- think clearer.
- handle stress with ease.
- feel healthier, both mentally and physically.
- connect more deeply with others.

You don't need a complete life overhaul to get there. Small, consistent practices—like breathing exercises, journaling, or mindful walks—can pave the way to that calm, clear-headed version of yourself.

Life's too short. It's time to quiet the noise and embrace the peace that comes with a calm mind.

Your Action Plan for a Calmer Mind

Now that we've covered the why behind calming your mind and the science-backed benefits, it's time to dive into the how. Creating a calmer mind doesn't require a complete lifestyle overhaul. It's about making small, sustainable changes that fit into your life—without adding more to your already full plate.

Here's a simple, step-by-step action plan to help you build a routine that calms your mind and strengthens your relationships.

Start Small: One Step at a Time

If you try to completely revamp your daily routine overnight, it's going to feel overwhelming. The key is to start small. Choose just one practice to begin with. Yep, just one.

Try this:

- **10-minute morning meditation:** Before checking your phone or diving into emails, sit somewhere quiet and focus on your breath. Even a few minutes can set a calmer tone for the day.
- **Nature walk during lunch:** Get outside and take a stroll. No podcasts, no scrolling—just you and the fresh air.
- **Evening brain dump:** Before bed, jot down your thoughts, worries, or to-dos to clear your head and make it easier to fall asleep.

Starting with one practice makes it doable. Once it becomes part of your routine, adding more feels natural—not forced.

Create a Routine: Anchor Calm to Existing Habits

We're creatures of habit, so the easiest way to build a new one is to anchor it to something you're already doing. Think of it as piggybacking your new calm-inducing habit onto an existing one.

For example:

- **Meditate after brushing your teeth:** You're already in the bathroom—just sit for 5–10 minutes after brushing.
- **Journal before bed:** Pair it with your nightly wind-down routine, maybe after you put on pajamas or set your alarm.
- **Mindful breathing before meals:** Take three deep breaths before you dig in. It helps ground you and improves digestion (bonus!).

Track Your Progress: Reflect and Adjust

We often don't notice subtle improvements until we track them. Reflecting on how your chosen practice impacts your mood and mindset helps you stay motivated—and shows you it's working.

Here's how to track:

- **Mood tracker:** Use a simple scale (1–5) to rate your stress or calmness levels each day.
- **Journaling prompts:** At the end of the week, ask yourself:
- *How did I feel after practicing?*
- *Did I notice fewer overthinking spirals?*
- *How did it affect my relationships?*

Build Variety: Mix It Up to Keep It Fresh

Once you've got one practice down, start adding variety. Different strategies work for different moods and triggers, so having options keeps things interesting and effective.

Mix and match:

- **Mindfulness plus movement:** Try yoga, tai chi, or even mindful hiking—moving your body while staying present.
- **Meditation plus journaling:** Start with a short meditation and follow it up with freewriting to clear your head.
- **Deep breathing plus nature therapy:** Practice focused breathing while sitting in a park or during a slow nature walk.

Having multiple tools means you can adapt based on your day. Feeling restless? Opt for a mindful walk. Super anxious? A grounding exercise like deep breathing might be better.

Prepare for Triggers: Have a Go-To Calm Plan

Overthinking often strikes when we least expect it—mid-meeting, during an argument, or even while trying to fall asleep. Having a plan for these moments is key.

Try these in-the-moment strategies:

- **Step away:** If you feel your mind spiraling, physically move—take a walk, go outside, or even switch rooms. Movement helps reset your mind.
- **Deep breathing:** Try the 4-7-8 technique—inhale for 4 seconds, hold for 7, exhale for 8. It helps calm your nervous system fast.
- **Grounding with 5-4-3-2-1:**
- 5 things you can see

- 4 things you can touch
- 3 things you can hear
- 2 things you can smell
- 1 thing you can taste

Celebrate Wins: Even the Tiny Ones Count

Progress isn't always huge or obvious, but every small win matters. Recognizing these moments reinforces your habit and keeps you motivated.

Celebrate when you

- paused before reacting in an argument.
- chose a mindful walk instead of scrolling Instagram.
- noticed you slept better after journaling before bed.

Keep a "calm wins" list in your journal or on your phone. Every time you catch yourself handling a situation better than before, write it down. Over time, you'll see just how far you've come.

Bringing It All Together:

By following this action plan, you're not just calming your mind—you're creating real, lasting change in your life and relationships.

Here's your roadmap:

1. Start small with one calming practice.

2. Anchor it to an existing habit to make it stick.
3. Track your progress to see the impact.
4. Add variety as you go to keep things fresh.
5. Prepare for triggers so overthinking doesn't derail you.
6. Celebrate your wins—because every step counts.

By the end of this journey, you'll feel more grounded, focused, and connected—to yourself and the people around you. Over-thinking won't disappear overnight, but with these tools, you'll be equipped to quiet the noise and embrace a calmer, clearer mind.

And hey, the fact that you're reading this and thinking about making a change? That's already a win worth celebrating.

Final Thoughts

Here you are—standing at the edge of real, meaningful change. You've learned how overthinking tangles up your mind, im-pacts your relationships, and messes with your peace. But more importantly, you now have the tools to untangle that mess. You know how to pause, breathe, and choose calm over chaos.

And that? That's powerful.

But even with a calm mind, we still face decisions that make us second-guess, spiral, or freeze up. Whether it's deciding how to respond during a tough conversation or choosing between two life paths, overthinking loves to sneak back in when choices feel heavy.

In the next chapter, we're diving into exactly how to hit the reset button on your decision-making process. We'll unpack why overthinking clouds your judgment, how to cut through the noise, and most importantly, how to make choices with clarity and confidence.

4

Chapter 4: The Decision-Making Reset

Chelsea had always prided herself on being thoughtful, but her boyfriend Brian often joked that she could turn choosing a sandwich into a life-altering event. While he laughed about it, Chelsea knew her overthinking was no joke—especially when it came to their relationship.

Take Brian's birthday dinner last year, for example. Chelsea wanted it to be perfect: the right restaurant, the ideal gift, and just the right words to make him feel special. But instead of planning with confidence, she spiraled.

She spent hours scrolling through restaurant reviews, texting friends for advice, and replaying conversations in her head to figure out if Brian had ever dropped a hint about his preferences. She picked a restaurant, then changed her mind. She ordered a gift but canceled it because it didn't feel personal enough. By the time his birthday rolled around, Chelsea was so consumed by the pressure to make everything perfect that she hadn't actually made any reservations or finalized her plans.

When the day arrived, Brian could tell something was off. At dinner—an awkward, last-minute pizza delivery at her apartment—he asked if she was okay. Chelsea, sobbing, confessed everything: How she'd worried so much about doing the wrong thing that she'd done nothing at all. Brian tried to reassure her, but Chelsea could see the disappointment in his eyes. She had missed the point—he just wanted to spend time with her, not have some grand, perfect evening. Yet, she was so stressed and consumed with overthinking that she couldn't enjoy being in the moment.

That night, Chelsea realized how much her overthinking was hurting their relationship. It wasn't just about birthdays; it was about how often she hesitated to share her feelings, made them late by rethinking outfits, or turned small disagreements into hours of silent stress. She wasn't fully present with Brian, and it was taking a toll on their love.

Determined to break free from the cycle, Chelsea started small. She learned about decision-making tools like the five-second rule. She also practiced trusting her gut by making quick calls on minor things—what to cook for dinner, which show to watch, or whether to speak up about something bothering her.

One day, Brian asked if she wanted to take a weekend trip. Normally, Chelsea would have agonized over the budget, itinerary, and what Brian might expect. Instead, she smiled and said, "Yes, let's do it," without overthinking.

That trip turned out to be one of their best weekends together. Without her usual mental baggage, Chelsea felt lighter and more connected to Brian. She found joy in the little things, like laughing at bad road trip snacks or dancing on the beach at sunset.

The decision reset didn't cure her overthinking immediately—it was about learning when to pause and when to act, especially in moments that mattered. Over time, Chelsea noticed her relationship was thriving. Brian seemed happier and more relaxed, and she was finally able to enjoy their time together without the weight of second-guessing every move.

For Chelsea, resetting her decision-making wasn't just about improving herself—it was about rediscovering the joy of being present in love. And Brian? He was just glad she finally picked a restaurant without reading 500 reviews.

This chapter is all about hitting the reset button on how you make decisions. Because overthinking isn't helping you—it's holding you hostage. And it's affecting the connections you care about most.

So, if you're tired of overanalyzing everything, stressing before making plans, or feeling stuck in your own head, let's reset together. It's time to make decisions with more ease, less stress, and way more connection.

Quick Decision-Making Frameworks

When emotions run high, making decisions can feel like trying to untangle Christmas lights that have been in storage for years. You know there's an end somewhere, but all you see is a tangled mess of wires. That's exactly how it feels when you're stuck deciding how to handle a disagreement with your partner, especially when overthinking takes the wheel.

Cue the pro-con list—a classic, simple tool that can work wonders if you know how to use it without spiraling into overanalyzing mode.

The Pro-Con List: Your Emotional GPS

The beauty of a pro-con list is that it gets everything out of your head and onto paper. It stops the endless loop of thoughts that sound like: *If I say this, they might think that, but if I don't say anything, will they think I'm avoiding it? And what if I'm just being too sensitive?* You get the idea.

Let's say you and your partner had a disagreement about how much time you're spending with friends lately. You're torn between letting it go (because conflict is exhausting) or bringing it up again (because it still bothers you). Here's how the pro-con list can help simplify that mental chaos:

- **Pros of bringing it up:**
- It clears the air and avoids long-term resentment.
- It gives both of us a chance to understand each other's feelings.
- It could strengthen communication in the relationship.
- **Cons of bringing it up:**
- It might escalate into another argument.

- It could make things awkward for a bit.
- I might get emotional and say something I don't mean.

Looks simple, right? But here's where overthinkers get tripped up—they start adding way too much to the list. Suddenly, it turns into a full-blown spreadsheet with subpoints, color-coding, and possible outcomes of each scenario (*If I bring it up on a Tuesday, will that make him more or less receptive?*).

Let's check out some tips to keep it simple:

- **Limit your list to five points per side:** Overanalyzing loves an open-ended project. Give it boundaries. Stick to five solid pros and cons. That's enough to see the big picture without drowning in details.
- **Focus on what matters most:** Not every point holds equal weight when emotions are involved. After listing your pros and cons, circle the one or two points on each side that matter most to you. This helps highlight what's really driving your decision.
- **Time-box it:** Give yourself a set time to make the list—like 10 minutes max. Set a timer if you need to. The goal is to capture your initial thoughts, not to perfect them.
- **Check for emotional bias:** Sometimes, we write what we want the list to say. If you find your cons are stacked a mile high compared to your pros, ask yourself: *Am I avoiding this because it's hard or because it's truly not worth it?*
- **Gut-check it:** After making the list, take a moment and notice how you feel. Often, your gut already knows the answer. If reading your pros made you feel a sense of relief or empowerment, that's a clue.

Using a pro-con list isn't about making the perfect decision—it's about moving forward with clarity rather than being stuck in the mental quicksand. And when it comes to handling emotionally charged situations, that clarity can be the difference between a calm, constructive conversation and one that starts with, "We need to talk..." and ends in tears.

So, the next time you're stuck in a decision loop, grab a pen, draw two columns, and let the pro-con List do its thing—just keep it simple, honest, and above all, kind to yourself.

The Five-Second Rule and The Two-Minute Rule: Your New Best Friends Against Overthinking

Ever had one of those moments where you know exactly what you should do, but five minutes later, you're still sitting there, replaying every possible outcome? Yep, that's overthinking in action—it loves to swoop in and hijack the moment before you can act. That's where the five-second rule and the two-minute rule come in. Think of them as the dynamic duo that helps you get out of your head and into action before self-doubt can say, "Hey, wait a minute..."

The Five-Second Rule: Stop Overthinking Before It Starts

The five-second rule, popularized by Mel Robbins, is beautifully simple: When you feel an instinct to act on something important, count backward from five—5-4-3-2-1—and then do it. No hesitating, no spiraling, no overanalyzing.

Let me paint a picture.

Erin had been stewing all morning over a heated argument with her husband. It wasn't a huge blow-up, but Erin said something snippy that she regretted almost immediately. She knew she needed to apologize, but the overthinking committee in her brain was already holding a meeting:

What if he's still mad?

What if my apology makes it worse?

Maybe I should wait until tomorrow... or next week?

Erin picked up her phone, scrolled to her husband's name (he was at work), and froze. That's when she remembered the five-second rule.

5-4-3-2-1—and before her brain could talk her out of it, she typed: "Hey, I'm really sorry about what I said earlier. I was out of line, and I value our relationship way more than my bad mood. Can we talk?"

Send.

Erin felt the anxiety bubble up, but it quickly deflated when he replied minutes later: "Thank you for this. I was upset, but I'm glad you reached out. Let's talk tonight."

That simple action—done before her inner overthinker could take over—saved Erin hours (if not days) of unnecessary stress.

The key here? Action beats overthinking. The five-second rule is like flipping a switch in your brain before self-doubt gets a chance to sabotage you. Use it when you know what needs to be done but feel the pull to hesitate—whether it's sending that apology, speaking up in a meeting, or even asking someone out for coffee.

The Two-Minute Rule for Small Decisions: Bye-Bye, Decision Fatigue

Now, for the smaller, everyday stuff that shouldn't drain your brainpower—but somehow does. Ever spent 20 minutes scrolling through Uber Eats only to end up eating toast for dinner because you couldn't decide? That's decision fatigue in action, and it's exhausting.

Enter the two-minute rule: If the decision won't affect your life in the long run (what to eat, what to watch, which coffee shop to go to), give yourself two minutes max to decide. That's it. Time's up—choose and move on.

Here's how it works in real life:

Julie and her husband, Dave, were notorious for falling into the "What do you want to eat?" black hole. It would start with innocent suggestions— "I'm good with anything!"—and end with both of them cranky, hungry, and still undecided.

One night, after way too long scrolling through takeout options, Julie pulled out her phone timer.

"Alright, we've got two minutes to decide dinner. Go!"

They went back and forth—pizza, sushi, Thai—until the timer buzzed. Julie blurted, "Sushi!" and that was that. No more endless debates.

The two-minute rule helps you stop over-prioritizing decisions that don't deserve that much mental energy. It's freeing, really. You'll be amazed at how much time and headspace you reclaim when you realize: *This choice doesn't need to be perfect—it just needs to be made.*

To sum it up:

- Use the five-second rule when emotions and self-doubt start creeping in—especially in decisions that involve vulnerability or courage.
- Use the two-minute rule for the everyday stuff that eats up way more time than it should.

Together, these two rules create a powerful filter: *Is this a quick decision? Two minutes. Is this an important but scary one? Five seconds to act before fear kicks in.*

The result? Less mental clutter, more confident choices, and—best of all—stronger, healthier relationships that don't get bogged down by indecision and overthinking.

Trusting Your Intuition: Rebuilding Confidence in Your Gut Instincts

You know that little voice inside you—the one that whispers, "Something feels off," or "Say thank you now," or even just, "Go with the blue shirt today"? That's your intuition. It's like your internal GPS, guiding you through life's twists and turns. But when you're an overthinker, that voice can get drowned out by the endless noise of what-ifs, maybes, and should-I-reallys?

Overthinking has a sneaky way of eroding trust in your natural instincts. You might second-guess your feelings, question your choices, or overanalyze simple decisions to the point where you can't tell the difference between fear, logic, or gut. It's like having a perfectly good compass but constantly spinning it around and wondering why you're lost.

But the good news? You can rebuild that trust in your intuition—because it's still there, waiting patiently for you to listen.

When Your Gut Gets It Right

Think about this: How many times have you walked into a room and immediately sensed that someone was upset—even before they said a word? Or maybe you've had that split-second instinct to send a "thinking of you" text, only to find out your friend was having a rough day. That's your intuition at work—

quiet, subtle, but often spot-on.

In relationships, our gut instincts are like emotional tuning forks. They pick up on energy, body language, and subtle shifts that our overthinking minds might miss. Like when

- you sense that your partner needs some space after a tough day, even if they say, "I'm fine."
- you feel an overwhelming urge to say, "I appreciate you," at the exact moment your loved one needs to hear it.
- you instinctively know when to step in during a heated conversation and when to hold back and let things cool down.

These moments show that your intuition already knows a lot about how to handle emotional connections—you just have to give it the floor again.

Practical Intuition Exercises: Strengthen Your Gut Muscle

Rebuilding trust in your intuition is like strengthening a muscle. The more you use it, the stronger it gets. Here are a few simple ways to start tuning back in:

- **The "First Instinct" game:** Start with low-stakes decisions. Next time you're picking out a gift, responding to a partner's question, or even deciding which movie to watch, go with your first instinct—no overthinking allowed. Notice how it feels to make a choice quickly and with confidence.

- **Morning check-in:** Before diving into your day, take 60 seconds to close your eyes and ask yourself: *What do I need most today?* Don't overanalyze—just notice the first thought or feeling that comes up. Maybe it's *I need a break* or *I need connection.* Let that guide one small action in your day.
- **The body compass:** Your body often knows the truth before your brain does. When faced with a decision, try this: Close your eyes, take a deep breath, and imagine saying yes to the choice. How does your body feel? Lighter? Tense? Then, imagine saying no and notice any shifts. This can help reveal what your intuition is already telling you.

Journal Prompts to Reflect on Your Intuition Wins

Writing things down helps solidify those "aha" moments. Here are some journal prompts to help you reflect on times your intuition served you well:

- *When was the last time I trusted my gut and it worked out? What happened?*
- *Have there been moments when I ignored my instincts and regretted it? What can I learn from that?*
- *What feelings or physical sensations usually show up when my intuition is guiding me?*
- *How can I practice listening to my gut more in my daily interactions, especially with loved ones?*

Rebuilding trust in your intuition isn't about making perfect decisions every time. It's about reestablishing that quiet confidence—the sense that you know what's best for you, even when your overthinking brain tries to convince you otherwise.

So, the next time you feel that little nudge—whether it's to speak up, reach out, or simply choose the blue shirt—listen. That's your gut, reminding you that it's still got your back.

When to Think More vs. Act: Striking the Right Balance

If you're an overthinker, you probably know the struggle of living in that awkward space between *Should I say something?* and *Maybe I should just let it go.* Sometimes, you need to pause and think things through, and other times, it's better to act without overcomplicating it. The trick? Knowing the difference.

In relationships, this balance is everything. It helps you avoid knee-jerk reactions that can hurt someone's feelings but also prevents you from missing moments that could strengthen your connection.

Knowing the Difference: When to Pause and When to Act

Let's circle back to Chelsea because, honestly, she's all of us.

Chelsea and her husband, Brian, had been arguing more than usual. One night, during dinner, Brian made a comment about how distracted she'd been lately. Without thinking, she snapped, "Well, maybe if you actually listened to me, I wouldn't be so distant!" The words flew out before she had a chance to filter them, and as soon as they landed, she regretted it.

This was a classic "pause before you speak" moment. Heated emotions often call for thoughtful deliberation. Taking a breath—or even saying, "I need a minute to think about how to respond"—can save you from saying something hurtful in the heat of the moment.

But then, there are times when acting fast is the better move.

A few days after that argument, Chelsea was scrolling through old photos and found one of their first trip together. She felt a warm rush of nostalgia and, without overthinking it, texted Brian:

"I know things have been tense lately, but I was just looking at this picture and remembered how much I love you. Let's plan another trip soon."

No analysis. No second-guessing. Just a spontaneous, heartfelt gesture. And you know what? It completely softened the tension between them.

The takeaway? Pause when emotions are high and words could do harm. Act quickly when a moment of connection or kindness presents itself—before overthinking talks you out of it.

Decision Filters: How to Know When to Think or Act

When you're stuck in decision limbo, use these simple filters to help guide your next move:

- *Does this decision significantly impact the relationship?*
- **Yes?** Take time to think it through. Big conversations—like discussing boundaries, handling conflicts, or making future plans—deserve careful consideration.
- **No?** If it's a low-stakes choice (what movie to watch, where to go for dinner), don't overthink it. Make a quick call and move on.
- *Will waiting improve the outcome or just add more stress?*
- **Waiting helps:** When emotions are high, giving yourself (and the other person) time to cool off can lead to a healthier, more productive conversation.
- **Waiting hurts:** If you're putting something off out of fear (sending that apology text, reaching out after a misunderstanding), it's better to act before anxiety builds.
- *Am I making this more complicated than it needs to be?*
- If you catch yourself overanalyzing every angle or playing out imaginary scenarios, that's a sign it's time to stop thinking and start doing.

Signs You're Overthinking (and What to Do About It)

Overthinking can feel sneaky, but there are some telltale signs that it's taken over:

- **Rehashing past conversations:** Ever replay a disagreement 47 times in your head, wondering if you should've said something different? Yep, that's overthinking.
- **Seeking endless advice:** If you've asked three friends, your mom, and even the barista for their opinion on whether you should text someone back... you might be overthinking.
- **Paralysis by analysis:** Spending so much time weighing options that you end up making no decision at all. (Hello, scrolling Netflix for an hour and then going to bed without watching anything.)

Alissa was debating whether to bring up how distant Russ had seemed lately. She replayed every recent conversation, analyzing his tone, his word choices, even his texting patterns (*Why did he say 'okay' instead of 'sounds good'? Is he mad?*). She called two friends to dissect it, but by the end of the week, she still hadn't said anything to Russ.

Eventually, her friend Sarah said, "Girl, you're overthinking this. Just ask him how he's feeling."

Alissa took the advice, asked Russ directly, and—surprise—it turned out he was stressed about work, not upset with her. Problem solved. Hours of overthinking? Totally unnecessary.

Thoughtful deliberation has its place, especially in emotionally charged moments where your words and actions carry weight. But immediate action is powerful when it comes to small gestures of love, kindness, and connection.

Here's your new mantra:

· Pause and think when emotions are high and stakes are significant.
· Act quickly when your gut tells you to reach out, show love, or make someone's day better.

The more you practice this balance, the easier it becomes to know when to slow down and when to jump in—without overthinking every move. And that, my friend, is how you build deeper, healthier, and more connected relationships.

Practical Decision Exercises: Building Confidence and Clarity

Let's face it—decision-making can feel like running a mental marathon when you're an overthinker. Even the tiniest choices (*Do I want coffee or tea?*) can spiral into an internal debate worthy of a courtroom drama. But here's the good news: Decision-making is a skill you can strengthen.

Just like training a muscle, the more you practice making decisions—big and small—the more confident and clear-headed you'll feel. And that clarity doesn't just make life easier for you; it can also ease tension in your relationships, where indecisiveness often leads to frustration or misunderstandings.

So, let's dive into some daily decision exercises to help you build that decision-making muscle and reduce overthinking, one choice at a time.

Micro-Decisions: The Fast-Choice Workout

Think of micro-decisions as your warm-up reps. These are the small, low-stakes choices that you can use to practice making quick decisions without overanalyzing.

The goal? To build confidence and show yourself that not every decision needs hours of deliberation.

Try this:

- What to wear today? Give yourself 60 seconds to choose an outfit—no outfit changes, no overthinking.
- Which snack to grab? Don't agonize over whether hummus or peanut butter is the healthier choice. Pick what sounds good and move on.
- What music to play? First playlist that pops up? Hit play.

These micro-decisions are simple, but they send a powerful message to your brain: "I can trust myself to choose quickly and move forward."

The Role-Reversal Exercise: Be Your Own Best Friend

When you're stuck in a decision spiral, sometimes the best thing you can do is step outside of yourself and see the situation from a fresh perspective.

Here's how:

- Imagine your friend is facing the same decision you're overthinking. What advice would you give them?
- Would you tell them to trust their gut? To stop overthinking? To go for it?

Melody was debating whether to reach out to her husband after a minor disagreement. She worried, *What if he's still mad? What if I say the wrong thing?*

But when she imagined her husband coming to her with the same situation, Melody knew exactly what she'd say: "Just send him a quick message. He'll appreciate the effort. Don't overthink it."

By flipping the script, Melody was able to make the decision with more clarity—and less emotional baggage.

Pro tip: If role-playing isn't enough, actually write yourself a note as if you were the friend giving advice. Seeing it in black and white often makes the right choice clearer.

The 30-Day Decision Journal: Track and Reflect

Want to build long-term trust in your decision-making? Start a 30-day decision journal—your personal record of daily decisions and how they impact your life and relationships.

Here's how it works:

- Every evening, jot down three decisions you made that day.

(Big or small—everything counts!)
- Write a quick note on how you made the choice. Was it instinctive? Thought-out? Did you overthink it?
- Reflect on the outcome. How did that decision impact your mood, your relationships, or your confidence?

Here's an example entry:

- Decision: Sent an apology text after an argument.
- Process: Used the five-second rule—typed it before I could overthink.
- Outcome: Partner responded positively. Felt relief and proud I didn't spiral.

By the end of 30 days, you'll start to see patterns—moments where intuition led you in the right direction, instances where overthinking tripped you up, and areas where you're building strength.

Practice "Good Enough" Decisions: The Art of Letting Go of Perfect

Here's a hard truth for overthinkers: No decision will ever be perfect—especially in relationships, where compromise is part of the deal.

That's why learning to make "good enough" decisions is such a game-changer.

What's a "good enough" decision? It's one that meets the

needs of the situation without needing to be the perfect choice. It values progress and harmony over perfection.

Let's revisit Chelsea and Brian. They were planning a date night but couldn't decide between two restaurants. After 20 minutes of back-and-forth, Chelsea finally said, "Let's go to the Italian place. It's good enough, and I'm hungry."

Guess what? The food was great, they had fun, and neither of them remembered the debate afterward.

Making "good enough" decisions can ease tension and promote harmony in relationships by

- reducing decision fatigue. Less time debating = more time enjoying.
- encouraging flexibility. Not every choice needs to be a hill to die on.
- fostering connection. It shows you're willing to compromise and prioritize time together over nitpicking details.

Practice tip: When faced with a low-stakes relationship decision (where to eat, what movie to watch, etc.), ask yourself this:

- *Will this choice really matter a week from now?*
- *Is this good enough to keep things moving and enjoyable?*

If the answer is yes, go with it and let go of the pressure to get it "just right."

Decision-making doesn't have to feel like carrying the weight of the world on your shoulders. By practicing small, daily choices, flipping perspectives, and embracing "good enough" decisions, you can build confidence in your ability to make choices quickly, clearly, and with less stress.

And here's the beautiful part: When you start trusting yourself more, your relationships benefit, too. Fewer debates over dinner plans, more spontaneous gestures of love, and way less time stuck in overthinking spirals.

So, grab your journal, make that quick snack choice, and remind yourself: progress over perfection—always.

Action Plan–Steps to Make Confident Decisions Quickly

Making decisions doesn't have to feel like climbing a mountain in flip-flops. With a simple plan, you can cut through the over-thinking and start making choices that feel clear, confident, and, most importantly, stress-free. This action plan will guide you through five practical steps to help you make decisions more quickly while building trust in yourself and improving your relationships along the way.

Step 1: Simplify Choices

Overthinking thrives on too many options. When faced with a decision, the first move is to narrow it down.

- **What to do:** Limit your options to two or three. Whether you're choosing a date night activity or deciding how to approach a tough conversation, fewer choices make it easier to move forward.

· **Example:** Instead of scrolling through dozens of dinner ideas, narrow it down: "Italian or sushi tonight?" That's it—no more.

Bonus tip: When in doubt, ask yourself: *Which option feels lighter or more exciting?* That's usually your gut guiding you.

Step 2: Set a Time Limit

Decisions expand to fill the time you give them. That's why setting a time limit forces clarity and reduces second-guessing.

· **What to do:** Decide how long you're willing to think about the decision—whether it's two minutes, five minutes, or an hour for bigger choices. Then, stick to it.
· **Example:** *I'll decide on a birthday gift in the next 10 minutes* or *I'll think about how to approach that tough conversation until lunch, then make a call.*

Pro tip: Use timers on your phone to keep yourself accountable. The countdown adds a sense of urgency that can help you avoid spiraling.

Step 3: Communicate Clearly

Even the best decisions can fall flat if they're poorly communicated. Learning how to express your choices to others helps avoid misunderstandings and shows confidence.

- **What to do:** Frame your decisions positively and invite collaboration, especially in relationships. Use language that includes the other person and explains your reasoning.
- **Example:** Instead of saying, "We're going to the movies," try: "I'd love for us to see that new comedy tonight—I think it'll be fun! What do you think?"

This approach shows that you've made a decision but are still considering their input, which builds connection and avoids coming across as controlling.

Pro tip: If the decision involves emotions or conflict (like discussing boundaries), use "I" statements: "I feel more comfortable if we..." This keeps things clear and avoids blame.

Step 4: Learn From Outcomes

No decision is perfect, and that's okay. The key is to see every choice as a learning opportunity, not a final verdict on your judgment skills.

- **What to do:** After making a decision, take a moment to reflect:
- *What worked?*
- *What would I do differently next time?*
- *Did this choice help me feel more connected or aligned with my values?*
- **Example:** Let's say you picked a restaurant your partner didn't love. Instead of thinking, *I always choose wrong,* reframe it: *Okay, next time I'll ask more about what they're in the mood for.*

Every decision teaches you something—it's just about paying attention.

Step 5: Celebrate Progress

Small wins are the stepping stones to big changes. Acknowledging your progress helps build momentum and rewires your brain to associate decision-making with success instead of stress.

- **What to do:** At the end of the day, reflect on a few decisions you made confidently—no matter how small.
- *I picked dinner without overthinking.*
- *I sent that tough text without waiting hours.*
- *I resolved that disagreement quickly and calmly.*
- **Example:** If you and your partner avoided a typical argument because you communicated your choice clearly, that's a win worth celebrating. Even choosing what movie to watch without a debate? That counts, too!

Pro tip: Consider keeping a "Decision Wins" list in your journal or on your phone. Over time, you'll see just how far you've come—and that's incredibly motivating.

By following these five steps, you'll start making decisions more confidently, with less second-guessing and more trust in yourself. And the best part? These steps don't just help you—they also strengthen your relationships by reducing misunderstandings, fostering connection, and easing the tension that overthinking often creates.

Here's your quick recap:

- **Simplify choices:** Narrow it down to two or three options.
- **Set a time limit:** Decide quickly to minimize spiraling.
- **Communicate clearly:** Express decisions in a way that builds connection.
- **Learn from outcomes:** Reflect and reframe, no judgment.
- **Celebrate progress:** Acknowledge every win, big or small.

Remember, decision-making doesn't have to be perfect—it just has to move you forward. And every time you make a choice with confidence, you're taking one more step toward letting go of overthinking and embracing clarity, ease, and connection.

Final Thoughts

You've made real progress—learning how to simplify choices, set time limits, trust your gut, and communicate clearly. Most importantly, you've seen that decisions don't have to be perfect; they just need to move you forward.

But what about when there's no clear answer? When uncertainty takes over and overthinking creeps back in? That's what we'll tackle next.

In the next chapter, you'll learn how to make confident choices even when the outcome is unclear. Because life isn't about having all the answers—it's about trusting yourself to move forward anyway. And you're more ready than you think.

5

Chapter 5: Taking Action Under Uncertainty

Overthinking can feel like a maze with no exit, especially when it starts affecting the moments that matter most in our relationships. Sometimes, even the simplest choices can become an obstacle when our minds are busy weighing every possibility. The story below is a familiar one for many of us. It captures the struggle of overthinking in a way that's both heartwarming and painfully relatable.

The Love Equation: Riley and Sam

Riley knew Sam was overthinking again. She could tell by the way Sam was staring at the restaurant menu as if it was a life-altering decision instead of a choice between tacos and pasta. Riley sighed and reached across the table, gently tapping Sam's fingers.

"Babe, if you think too hard, we'll be eating breakfast here instead of dinner."

Sam exhaled, finally putting the menu down. "I just... want to make the right choice."

"You know what the right choice is? Food. Any food. We're hungry. Pick one."

Sam smiled but still hesitated. This was classic Sam—an overthinker at heart. Decisions, no matter how small, had to be analyzed, weighed, and cross-examined before any action was taken. It was part of what Riley loved about him. Sam was thoughtful, always considering every possibility. But sometimes, that thoughtfulness turned into paralysis.

And lately, it wasn't just about dinner.

The Bigger Question

Riley swirled the straw in her drink, debating whether to bring up "The Conversation" again. They had been together for five years. Five years of amazing adventures, laughter, and spontaneous road trips—well, not so spontaneous.

Sam needed at least a month to "research" before agreeing to anything. Riley wanted to take the next step. She wanted a future—maybe a wedding, maybe kids, definitely a home filled with their kind of chaos.

But every time she brought it up, Sam clammed up, spiraling

into what-ifs. "What if we regret it? What if we're not financially stable enough? What if we change? What if we fail?"

Riley had run out of ways to say, "We'll figure it out." No matter how much reassurance she gave, Sam still couldn't make a decision.

Tonight, Riley decided, she was going to try a different approach. "Sam, can I ask you something?" Riley said, leaning in.

Sam nodded, sipping nervously from his drink.

"You worry a lot, right?"

"Understatement of the year," Sam muttered.

"So, let's break this down. What exactly are you worried about when it comes to us getting married or having kids?"

Sam rubbed his temples. "I just... what if we get married, and then down the line, things change? What if we're not as happy as we are now? What if we struggle? What if I'm not ready?"

Riley nodded. "Okay, let's play a game. Out of all those worries, which ones do you actually have control over?"

Sam blinked. "What?"

"Like, let's take 'What if we're not as happy as we are now?'

97

Can you control that?"

"I mean... I guess I can work on our relationship, communicate, make an effort."

"Exactly! That's problem-solving. But 'What if things change?' You can't control that. Life changes. We change. It's not a problem to solve; it's just a fact."

Sam was quiet.

Riley could see the gears turning.

"I just feel like overthinking helps me be prepared," Sam admitted.

"Prepared for what?" Riley asked gently. "Because worrying isn't the same as problem solving. If you're thinking about real, solvable things—like, say, how we'll balance finances together—that's useful. But running through every possible worst-case scenario? That just keeps you stuck."

Sam let out a deep breath. "So, you're saying... I need to stop trying to control things I can't and focus on what I can?"

"Ding ding ding! We have a winner!" Riley grinned.

Sam shook his head, laughing softly. "I love that you make things sound so simple."

"Because sometimes, they are. And for the record? I love you.

But I can't keep waiting for you to make up your mind about us."

Sam looked at her, really looked at her, and Riley saw something shift in his expression. "You're right," Sam finally said. "I don't want to let my fear keep us from moving forward. Maybe we don't have all the answers, and we never will. And maybe... that's okay."

Riley beamed. "That's more than okay. That's life, babe." And for the first time in months, Sam stopped overthinking for some time.

This story is a gentle reminder that while our minds may be wired to overanalyze every decision, sometimes life demands that we simply take a leap—even when uncertainty is the only guarantee. In moments of doubt, focusing on what we can control (like choosing to enjoy a meal or nurturing a relationship) can open the door to growth, connection, and progress.

In this chapter, we're going to explore how to change that overthinking into decisive, positive action. We'll uncover strategies you can use for accepting the unknown, trusting yourself, and finding clarity even when all the answers seem to be just out of reach. If you've ever found yourself stuck in a loop of what-ifs and unknowns, I see you. Let's dive into how you can start making choices confidently—even if they're not perfect—and build a life that's full of both spontaneity and meaningful direction.

Embracing Imperfect Action: Why Starting Messy Is Better Than Not Starting

Embracing imperfect action means giving yourself permission to start—even when everything isn't picture-perfect. There you are, standing on the edge of a diving board, heart pounding because you're waiting for the water to look just right. But waiting for perfection only keeps you stuck. You can find yourself never diving in.

Perfectionism as Avoidance

It's easy to fall into the trap of believing you must be completely ready before taking any step forward. Like that friend who spent months preparing for a small art show, obsessing over every detail until nothing ever got painted. The truth is, perfectionism is often a form of avoidance. Instead of moving forward and learning through experience, we cling to the idea that we must have it all figured out first—a mindset that only deepens our fear of failure.

Worry: A Distraction, Not a Solution

There's a curious trick our minds play on us: When we worry, it temporarily eases our anxiety by making us feel like we're addressing the issue. For a brief moment, running through every potential obstacle feels productive. But this isn't true problem-solving. True problem-solving is about evaluating a situation, coming up with concrete steps, and then acting on them.

Worry, on the other hand, is like walking in circles—it distracts you from your emotions and ultimately leaves you no more prepared for challenges than before. Think about the times you've spent spiraling over worst-case scenarios; no matter how long you worry, the outcomes remain unchanged.

Messy Action Beats No Action

Every success story starts with a first, imperfect step. Think about all those writers staring at a blank page, terrified that their first draft won't be perfect. Yet, it's that initial, messy attempt that sets the stage for revisions, improvements, and eventual brilliance.

When you take action—no matter how rough around the edges—you open yourself up to growth and learning. That small, imperfect move is far more valuable than standing still in the pursuit of perfection.

Lowering the Stakes and Embracing the 70% Rule

Most decisions aren't life-or-death; they're stepping stones that build clarity and confidence. Lowering the stakes means recognizing that most choices are reversible and provide opportunities to adjust as you go. If you're 70% sure about a decision, that might be all the certainty you really need. Waiting for 100%

only leads to endless hesitation.

For instance, think of someone who hesitated to join a community class, worrying they weren't an expert enough. When they finally took the leap with a 70% conviction, they discovered not only a new skill but also a supportive community that welcomed them as they learned and grew.

Progress doesn't demand perfection—it demands action. When you understand that perfectionism is just a disguise for our fears and that worry rarely brings real solutions, you can shift your focus to taking those messy, imperfect steps.

Remember, starting is often the most important part. So, if you're 70% sure about something, lean into it. Welcome the messiness, learn from every stumble, and discover that moving forward—even imperfectly—is the surest path to growth.

Managing Fear of Failure: Reframing Failure as a Learning Opportunity

Managing the fear of failure means shifting your focus from dread to curiosity—seeing each stumble as a valuable lesson rather than a catastrophe.

Failure Is Data, Not Disaster

Take Beth, for example. Beth loved to bake and decided to try a new cake recipe. The first time, her cake came out too dry, and the frosting was off. Instead of seeing it as a disaster, she treated it as a data point: a clue that she needed to adjust the baking time and tweak the ingredient ratios. Each misstep taught her what worked and what didn't, gradually leading her to perfect her recipe.

Reframing Setbacks: Ask, What Did I Learn?

Then there's Rob. He once launched an online store with high hopes, only to find that his initial marketing strategy wasn't attracting customers. His first reaction was to feel defeated. But rather than dwell on what he lost, Rob shifted his focus and asked, *What did I learn?* He discovered that his target audience was different from what he had assumed and refined his approach accordingly. By reframing the setback, Rob turned a disappointing outcome into progress toward future success.

The Five-Year Perspective: Most Failures Won't Matter in the Long Run

Beth experienced several baking mishaps early on, and each one discouraged her. Yet, when she looked back over the past five years, she realized those failures were just temporary bumps along the process. They didn't define her progress. Instead, they provided essential insights that eventually led her to create delightful desserts. This long-term view reminds us that most setbacks are minor in the grand scheme of our lives.

Fear as Proof You Care

Rob often felt a flutter in his stomach before launching new products. That nervousness wasn't a sign of weakness; it was proof that he cared deeply about his business. Each time he stepped out of his comfort zone, that fear reminded him he was pushing his boundaries and growing. Much like learning to ride a bike—where the initial wobbles eventually give way to balance and confidence—Rob understood that fear was a natural part of the journey toward improvement.

In the end, managing the fear of failure is about embracing the messy, unpredictable path of growth. Just like Beth and Rob, every imperfect attempt, every moment of worry, and every setback provides crucial feedback that paves the way for future success.

So, the next time you hesitate because you're scared of failing, remember: Each failure is simply a lesson in disguise—a small step on the long road to becoming your best self.

Building Confidence With Small Wins: The Power of Incremental Progress

Building confidence is a path made up of small, deliberate steps—each one building on the last until you find yourself standing taller than before.

Confidence Is Earned, Not Innate

Take Lily, for example. She once believed that confidence was something you were either born with or you weren't. But when she decided to join a local book club, she discovered that every conversation she joined and every idea she shared built her confidence bit by bit. It wasn't a flash of brilliance at a single moment; it was a gradual process of showing up and learning from each experience.

Small Wins Create Momentum

Then there's Alex. When he first started his freelance graphic design work, he wasn't sure if he was good enough. Instead of waiting for a perfect project to prove his skills, Alex set small, achievable goals. Sometimes, this was finishing a quick logo sketch or successfully meeting a tight deadline. Every little win added up. With each completed project, his self-trust grew, eventually propelling him to take on larger and more challenging assignments.

Track Your Progress

Both Lily and Alex found that keeping track of their progress made a huge difference. Lily began keeping a simple journal where she noted every positive interaction and every small achievement—even if it was just sharing a thought during a club meeting.

Alex maintained a list of completed projects and client praises, which served as a visual reminder of how far he'd come. Looking back at these records helped them see tangible proof of their growth, especially on days when self-doubt crept in.

These are great ideas you, too, can implement!

Use "Done" Energy to Fuel Future Steps

There's a special kind of energy that comes from finishing something, even if it isn't perfect. After completing each journal entry or project, Lily and Alex took a moment to reflect on their wins. That "done" energy wasn't just a pat on the back; it became the fuel that pushed them to take on the next challenge, no matter how small. Celebrating these wins allowed them to build momentum that made future challenges seem less daunting.

In the end, building confidence isn't about waiting for one big breakthrough moment. It's about earning it with every small step you take, every little win you celebrate, and every bit of progress you track along the way. Just like Lily and Alex, you can harness the power of incremental progress to create lasting, self-assured change.

Action-Oriented Mindset: Tools for Moving Forward Despite Fear

Overthinking can feel like a heavy cloud, especially when it starts to impact our relationships. But what if we could shift gears—from getting stuck in doubt to taking action, even when fear is whispering in our ear? Let's explore how to train your mind to focus on solutions rather than obstacles and how a simple exercise can help you move forward despite the fear.

Overthinking vs. Action Thinking

Imagine your mind standing at a fork in the road. One path leads to overthinking—a place where you get tangled in worries and possibilities, endlessly analyzing problems without finding solutions. The other path, action thinking, is all about spotting opportunities, generating ideas, and taking even the smallest step forward. When you choose the action-oriented path, you empower yourself to address challenges head-on instead of feeling paralyzed by them.

A Quick Five-Minute Exercise to Get You Started

Try this simple exercise to shift your mindset from overthinking to action:

1. **Set a timer for five minutes:** Find a quiet spot where you won't be interrupted. Sit comfortably, take a deep breath,

and set a timer for five minutes.

2. **Identify an obstacle:** Spend the first minute reflecting on something that's been weighing on your mind. It might be an issue in your relationship, a personal challenge, or a decision you've been avoiding.

3. **Write it down:** For one minute, jot down your thoughts about the obstacle. Let everything flow without judgment—no need to filter or organize your ideas now.

4. **Shift to solutions:** Now, for the next three minutes, switch your focus. Write down as many solutions or steps as you can think of to tackle the obstacle. Be creative and let your ideas flow. This is your moment to think about possibilities rather than problems.

5. **Commit to one action:** Finally, choose one small action from your list that you can take today. Whether it's sending that text, having a conversation, or simply taking a moment to breathe, commit to that action.

And here's a little bonus: Try incorporating the five-second rule by Mel Robbins from the previous chapter. When you feel doubt creeping in, count down from five and then take that action before hesitation takes over.

Exercise: Would Future Me Thank Me?

Sometimes, a simple shift in perspective can ignite the motivation you need. This exercise is designed to help you prioritize actions that your future self will be grateful for. Get started by trying the following:

1. **Reflect on future you:** Close your eyes for a moment and picture yourself one year from now. Imagine what your life looks like, how you feel, and what you've accomplished.

2. **Identify a current challenge:** Open your eyes and think about a challenge or decision you're facing today. It could be something personal, relational, or a goal you've been putting off.

3. **Ask yourself the question:** Write down this question: "Would future me thank me for the choice I'm about to make?"

4. **List possible actions:** Spend the next two minutes listing out all the choices you can make regarding this challenge. For each option, consider whether it aligns with the kind of life your future self would appreciate. Be honest with yourself.

5. **Choose one action to take today:** From your list, pick one action that feels both manageable and meaningful. It might be something small—a phone call, a meeting, or even a simple decision that moves you in the right direction.

6. **Commit to it:** Write down your chosen action and commit to taking it within the next 24 hours. Let the thought that your future self will thank you fuel your motivation.

Remember, waiting for the perfect moment often means never starting at all. Every small action builds momentum, and each step forward brings clarity. By choosing an action-oriented mindset, you're not only solving problems—you're building a future that you'll be proud of. So, take a deep breath, trust your process, and start moving forward today.

Action Plan: Exercises to Build Courage and Act in Uncertainty

Taking action during uncertainty shouldn't focus on leaping without looking—it's about building courage through small, deliberate steps that slowly shift your mindset. Here's an action plan with practical exercises to help you move forward, even when fear is knocking at your door.

The Bold Action Challenge

Sometimes, we get caught in a loop of overthinking that stops us from doing anything at all. Take, for example, Jenna. She had been mulling over the idea of reaching out to a long-lost friend for months. Every time she thought about it, self-doubt held her back. One day, she decided to take the bold action challenge. She picked one thing she'd been overthinking—in this case, sending that message—and committed to taking one step within the next 24 hours. By doing so, Jenna broke the cycle of hesitation and reignited a meaningful connection. This challenge shows that even a small act of courage can shift the momentum of your life.

Now it's your turn!

Fear as Excitement Reframe

Have you ever noticed how your heart races before a big presentation or when you're about to try something new? That flutter isn't just fear—it's excitement in disguise. Consider Leo, who was nervous about asking for a promotion at work. Instead of letting his nerves hold him back, he reframed his physical sensations as excitement. Leo reminded himself that the same energy fueling his nerves could also power his ambition. When he shifted his perspective, he was able to step confidently into the conversation, knowing that his feelings were simply a natural response to an opportunity for growth.

It's important for you to be mindful that nervousness and excitement feel the same within your body.

The Regret Test

It's easy to stay stuck in our comfort zones when the thought of failure looms large. But what if you asked yourself a simple question: *How would future me thank me for taking this step?*

Carla, for instance, faced a decision about whether to apply for a job in a field she was passionate about but intimidated by. She paused and conducted her own regret test. Carla visualized her future self—one year down the road—and realized that not trying might lead to long-lasting regret. That insight pushed her to submit the application, setting her on a new, exciting career path.

The regret test helps remind you that the pain of missing out often outweighs the fear of stepping into the unknown.

Daily Micro-Actions

Significant changes often start with tiny steps. Think about Mike, who wanted to improve his fitness but felt overwhelmed by the idea of a major lifestyle overhaul. Instead of waiting for the perfect time or a grand plan, he committed to daily micro-actions.

Mike decided to do something small daily—a one-minute stretching routine, a short walk, or simply drinking an extra glass of water. Over time, these micro-actions built momentum, slowly changing his habits and boosting his confidence.

When you start with small, manageable decisions, you create a chain reaction that can lead to real, lasting change.

Each of these exercises serves as a tool to break free from the paralysis of overthinking. They're designed to help you build courage step by step, changing uncertainty into a pathway toward growth and success. So pick one, commit to it today, and remember: Every small action is a victory on the journey to a braver, more fulfilled you.

Final Thoughts

As we wrap up this chapter, take a moment to reflect on the path you've just traveled. We explored how overthinking can trap us in a cycle of doubt, and we discovered that action—imperfect, sometimes messy, but always forward-moving—is the antidote. We learned that every small win, every courageous step, and every shift in perspective builds the kind of confidence that propels us out of our comfort zones. Remember how Jenna reached out despite her doubts, how Leo transformed nervousness into excitement, and how Mike's daily micro-actions eventually reshaped his habits? These stories aren't just examples—they're proof that change is possible when we choose to act despite uncertainty.

Now, imagine having a toolkit ready for those moments when overthinking starts creeping back in—a set of real strategies you can pull out when you need that extra boost to move forward. That's exactly what our next chapter is all about.

In the upcoming chapter, we'll dive into tangible tools and quick fixes that will help you manage those overwhelming moments and keep your momentum going. Take a deep breath, celebrate the progress you've made, and get ready to equip yourself with the essential resources to tackle overthinking head-on. Your future self will thank you!

6

Chapter 6: The Overthinking Emergency Kit

Roger sighed as he looked down at his shopping cart—half full and yet somehow, three hours had passed. He rubbed his temples, staring at two nearly identical jars of pasta sauce, feeling his pulse quicken. *Organic or locally sourced? Less sugar or lower sodium? Which one would Sandra have picked?* He wasn't with Sandra anymore, hadn't been for months, but his brain still ran the same exhausting loops.

If I choose the wrong one, will dinner taste bad? Will it ruin the meal? What if I don't even like it? What if I get home and regret it?

He shook his head, frustrated. It's just sauce. Pick one and move on.

But this was how his mind worked. Every decision—big or small—felt like it carried the weight of the world. It wasn't just grocery shopping. Holidays were a nightmare. He would spend months agonizing over Christmas gifts for his family, only to second-guess himself up until the moment they opened them. At work, one email could send him into an anxious spiral, rereading it ten times before hitting send. And in relationships? His partners—both of his ex-wives—had taken the brunt of his stress, frustration, and indecisiveness.

It wasn't until his latest therapist pointed it out that Roger truly understood— overthinking was running his life. Worse, it was ruining it.

When his therapist first asked him to track his overthinking patterns, Roger resisted. *It's just how I am*, he thought. *I'm a detail-oriented person. What's wrong with that?*

But as he started paying attention, he realized it wasn't just thinking things through—it was spiraling. And when he spiraled, it was never just about the situation at hand. Grocery shopping wasn't just about groceries. It was about making the right choice.

Holidays weren't just about giving—it was about proving he knew his family, that he was thoughtful, that he wasn't going to let them down.

The weight of every decision—every interaction—was exhausting. And whoever was closest to him at the time? They got the worst of it.

His therapist introduced him to thought interruption techniques, tools designed to break the loop before he got lost in it. However, it took some time to find what worked for him.

Deep breathing? Didn't work. The moment he closed his eyes, his mind went into overdrive. Visualization? Same problem. The second he tried to picture a peaceful beach, his brain started asking, *What beach? What time of year? What temperature is the water?*

Nothing was clicking—until he stumbled upon two game-changers.

One day, after a particularly overwhelming work meeting, Roger's hands were clammy, his head spinning from analyzing every word he had said. He walked into the office kitchen, grabbed a glass of ice water, and pressed it to his forehead. Instantly, something shifted. The cold grounded him. It snapped him out of his thoughts.

He experimented with it more. At home, he started jumping into the shower when he felt himself spiraling, gradually lowering the temperature. The shock of cold forced him back into his body, out of his head. If he was at work, he'd chew on ice or squeeze an ice cube in his palm—just enough discomfort to break the loop.

He started keeping a travel mug full of ice on his desk at all times.

His therapist had suggested journaling, but Roger had resisted. *I'm not a diary guy,* he thought.

But one evening, after sitting in his car for 45 minutes debating whether to go into the gym (*What if I look stupid? What if I use the wrong machine?*), he grabbed an old receipt from the glove compartment and scribbled down every single thought racing through his head. He wrote fast, not worrying about grammar or making sense. Just dumping it all out.

And suddenly... he could breathe again.

That moment changed everything. He started keeping notebooks everywhere—one at work, one at home, one in his car. He even had a "Notes" file in his phone called "OT Book" (short for "Overthinking Thoughts"). Whenever his mind became too loud, he'd grab the closest notebook and scribble everything out—not to analyze, not to fix, just to release.

At work, he'd jot down intrusive thoughts in a notebook instead of letting them take over. In the car, if his brain was looping about something he said earlier that day, he'd dump it onto paper before going inside. At home, he made it a habit to "brain dump" before bed so he didn't carry his thoughts into the night.

He learned that the words didn't have to make sense—they just had to get out of his head.

Roger wasn't "cured." Overthinking was still part of him. But now, he had tools. When he felt himself getting lost in his thoughts, he had a plan. And for the first time in his life, decisions started getting easier.

Grocery shopping? Under 30 minutes. Holiday gifts? He set a two-hour limit and stuck to it. Work stress? Instead of overanalyzing every email, he sent them after one reread.

And in relationships? He was present in a way he had never been before.

Roger had spent his whole life believing that overthinking kept him safe, that analyzing every possibility prevented mistakes. But in the end, it had only robbed him of time, connection, and peace of mind.

Now? He still thought things through—but he didn't live in his thoughts anymore.
 And that made all the difference.

Welcome to the chapter designed for those moments when your mind feels like it's on overdrive, especially when those spiraling thoughts start to impact the relationships you care about.

It's time to find balance and create space for the connections that truly matter. Let's unpack these tools together so you can manage your inner world with more confidence, clarity, and kindness.

Stop-Overthinking Techniques: Immediate Tools to Get Unstuck

Overthinking can feel like your mind is stuck on a merry-go-round, but there are quick, real-world techniques that help you break the cycle. Here are some relatable strategies that work:

· **The five-minute decision rule:** Amy once spent ages

deciding which outfit to wear to her friend's birthday party. She asked herself, *Will this choice matter in five years?* Realizing it wouldn't, she set a five-minute timer. When the timer went off, Amy picked an outfit and enjoyed her evening without regret. This rule is a great reminder to save your mental energy for decisions that truly count.

· **Set a worry timer:** Mike often found himself lost in thought about work issues late at night. Instead of letting these worries haunt him all evening, he set a 10-minute "worry timer." During those 10 minutes, he allowed himself to mull over his concerns. When the timer rang, Mike consciously shifted his focus to relaxing activities, preventing his worries from taking over his night.

· **The *Will This Matter?* test:** When Sophie caught herself stressing over a minor mistake in an email, she paused and asked herself, *Will this still matter in a week? A month?* The answer was a clear no, and that simple test helped her let go of unnecessary stress, reminding her that not every hiccup deserves her full attention.

· **Name it to tame it:** Sometimes, simply calling out what's happening can diffuse its power. John noticed he was spiraling into overthinking and calmly said, "I'm overthinking right now." By naming it, he created a small distance between himself and his thoughts, making it easier to step back and regain control.

· **The one-word focus trick:** Emily chose the word "breathe" as her anchor. Whenever her mind began racing with worries or doubts, she'd repeat "breathe" to herself. This one-word trick served as a mental reset, pulling her back to the present moment and calming her spiraling thoughts.

These techniques are designed to give you practical, immediate tools to stop the overthinking loop. Experiment with them to see which best suits your life. Remember, it's not about silencing your thoughts completely but about finding balance and clarity so you can focus on what really matters.

Grounding Exercises: Using the Five Senses to Stay Present

Grounding exercises help you shift your focus from anxious thoughts to the physical sensations of the here and now. They remind you that you're not alone in your head—you have a body that can help ground you. Here are some techniques, complete with real-life examples to show how they work:

- **Quick journaling:** Amy found herself overwhelmed by swirling thoughts before an important presentation. She kept a small notebook handy and spent just a few minutes writing down her anxieties. By putting her thoughts on paper, Amy discovered that they felt less powerful and easier to manage. This expressive writing helped her clear her mind and organize her emotions, making it easier to move forward.
- **Cold water reset:** Think of Michael, who sometimes felt trapped in a cycle of negative thinking late at night. On one particularly rough evening, he splashed cold water on his face and even held an ice cube for a moment. The sudden chill acted like a reset button, snapping him out of his rumination and bringing his focus back to the present moment.

- **The "Describe It" technique:** When Sophie's mind began to spiral during a stressful day, she started to verbally describe her surroundings. "I see a soft blue cushion, a bright red mug, and a patterned rug that feels cozy," she would say. This simple exercise of detailing the textures, colors, and objects around her helped pull her attention away from her worries and back into the reality of her environment.

- **Engage your body:** John often felt tension building up when his thoughts got too heavy. He found that doing a quick stretch, shaking out his hands, or simply pressing his feet firmly into the floor brought him back into his body. These small movements served as reminders that he was here, in control, and not defined by his anxious thoughts.

Each of these exercises uses your senses to break the cycle of overthinking and ground you in the present moment. Experiment with them to see which resonates best with you, and remember—sometimes, the simplest physical actions can create the most significant mental shifts.

Thought Interruption Strategies: Break the Loop Mid-Thought

Thought interruption strategies help you break the loop mid-thought—interrupting those repetitive negative cycles before they overwhelm you and replacing them with something productive. Here are some actionable techniques, along with relatable examples:

- **Pattern disruption:** When Amy notices that she's spiraling into overthinking while sitting at her desk, she simply stands up and moves to another room or does a quick stretch. Even a brief change in scenery, like a short walk to the kitchen, can disrupt that negative cycle and give her mind a fresh perspective.
- **The *What's the Opposite?* question:** Imagine Mike is stuck on the thought, *I'm not good enough.* He pauses and asks himself, *What's the opposite belief?* This might lead him to recognize, *I have strengths, and I learn from my mistakes.* By exploring the counter-thought, Mike can replace his negative self-talk with a more balanced view.
- **Sing it out loud:** Sophie found that when her worries started to spiral, she would lighten the mood by saying her concern in a cartoonish voice or even singing it to a silly tune. This playful approach helps her detach emotionally from the worry, transforming an overwhelming thought into something less intimidating.
- **Rubber band snap:** John keeps a small rubber band on his wrist. Whenever he feels caught in a loop of negative thinking, he lightly snaps it against his skin. This gentle physical reminder signals a mental reset, helping him break free from the spiraling thought and refocus on the present.

Each of these strategies offers a way to step in mid-thought and redirect your mental energy. Experiment with these techniques to see which ones resonate best with you, and remember—the goal is to reclaim control and create space for more productive, positive thoughts.

Quick-Reset Meditations: Guided Practices for Mental Resets

Quick-reset meditations offer you a set of simple, guided practices that help clear the mental clutter and restore calm in just a few moments. These techniques are like a mental pit stop—short, intentional breaks that give you an opportunity to reset, regain clarity, and move forward with a refreshed mind. Here's a closer look at some of these practices with relatable examples:

- **Butterfly breathing (4-4-4-4):** When Amy feels overwhelmed during a busy workday, she changes her breathing into a graceful, calming ritual—just like a butterfly. She starts by gently inhaling for 4 seconds, imagining her wings slowly opening as she takes in the fresh air. Then, she holds her breath for 4 seconds, as if her butterfly is momentarily at rest on a flower. Next, she slowly exhales for 4 seconds, visualizing her wings closing softly, and finally holds again for 4 seconds before repeating the cycle. This rhythmic, fluttering pattern not only slows her racing thoughts but also grounds her firmly in the present. With each cycle, Amy feels her stress melting away, just as a butterfly emerges peacefully into the light.
- **The "Let It Float" visualization:** Mike's mind is swirling with worries before a big presentation. He closes his eyes and visualizes tying each anxious thought to a balloon, watching as it gently floats up into the sky. This mental imagery helps him detach from the intensity of his thoughts, allowing them to float away naturally.

- **10-second gratitude pause:** When Sophie finds herself caught in a spiral of negative thoughts, she takes a brief pause. She closes her eyes and quickly names three things that made her smile or laugh recently. Sometimes, this can be something she saw online, delicious food she ate, or even feeling the sun on her face. In just 10 seconds, this gratitude practice shifts her focus from what's troubling her to the positive aspects of her life.
- **Mantra reset:** John often feels his mind being hijacked by anxious thoughts. To reclaim his peace, he repeats a calming mantra, such as "I choose peace" or "This moment is enough." Each repetition reinforces a sense of calm and provides a counterbalance to his worries, helping him regain control of his mental space.
- **Music and sound therapy:** Sometimes, all it takes is the right song to change your mood. Studies show that listening to soothing music can offer immediate relief from stress (Victor, 2023). For example, when Emily feels overwhelmed, she puts on her favorite calming track. The gentle rhythms and harmonies create a mental safe space that drowns out the noise of her anxiety and helps her reconnect with a sense of inner calm.

Sometimes, a few seconds of mindful pause can make all the difference.

Action Plan: Create Your Own Emergency Kit for Overthinking Episodes

Creating your own emergency kit for overthinking is about tailoring a set of strategies that you can rely on when your thoughts start to spiral. This action plan is your personal toolkit, a way to be proactive and kind to yourself when you need a mental reset. Here's how you can build it:

- **Choose your top three tools:** Think about the techniques that have helped you in the past. For example, maybe Amy found that butterfly breathing, the "let it float" visualization, and the one-word focus trick work wonders for her. Choose the three strategies that resonate most with you and make a commitment to use them when you notice overthinking creeping in.
- **Make a quick-access reminder:** Keep your chosen strategies top of mind. Write them down on a sticky note, set them as your phone wallpaper, or jot them on an index card that you carry with you. You can even set reminders on your phone. Mike has his overthinking emergency kit saved as a note on his phone, and whenever he feels overwhelmed, he quickly pulls up his reminder and knows exactly what to do.
- **Set a "break the loop" alarm:** A daily reminder can help you check in with yourself before overthinking takes over. Picture Sophie setting an alarm labeled "break the loop" during her lunch break. When it goes off, she takes a moment to pause, evaluate her thoughts, and decide if it's time to use one of her grounding techniques.

- **Accountability partner:** Sometimes, sharing your plan with a friend can make all the difference. John teamed up with a close friend, and they agreed to remind each other to use their emergency kits during stressful times. This support system not only keeps you accountable but also makes the process feel less isolating.

When you create your own kit for overthinking, you're taking a proactive step toward a more balanced, mindful way of handling stress. Experiment with these steps, tailor them to your unique needs, and soon you'll have a go-to strategy list that helps you regain clarity and calm whenever overthinking strikes.

Final Thoughts

You've now got a set of practical, personal tools that will help you regain control when overthinking starts taking over. Use the techniques we've explored and start breaking the cycle, calm your mind, and create space for clarity and connection.

Remember, these steps are all about progress and building a healthier relationship with your mind. When you keep these tools within arm's reach, you'll be ready to take on overthinking head-on, anytime it strikes. Now that you have your emergency kit in place, it's time to go even deeper.

In the next chapter, we'll focus on building lasting mental freedom habits. We will look at those small, consistent actions that can unlock even greater peace and resilience in your daily life. Get ready to step beyond just managing overthinking and into the space of true mental freedom.

It's time to welcome a life where your thoughts serve you, not control you.

7

Chapter 7: Building Mental Freedom Habits

Leila and Micah had been married for ten years. Ten years of love, laughter, and inside jokes that only they understood. But also, ten years of late-night debates over what he meant by that or why she took so long to respond. Ten years of playing mental chess, trying to predict each other's reactions, and—if they were being really honest—ten years of exhausting themselves with what-if scenarios that rarely ever came true.

They loved each other. That was never the issue. The issue was their minds, which were constantly working overtime, turning minor situations into full-blown mental marathons. And after a decade of going in circles, they finally agreed: Something had to change.

Over the years, overthinking had created unnecessary arguments, silent treatments, and emotional exhaustion.

There was text message anxiety. If Micah didn't text Leila back within a reasonable amount of time, her mind would spiral. *Is he mad? Did I say something wrong?* Meanwhile, Micah, oblivious to the panic on the other end, was just in the middle of a meeting.

There was post-argument analysis paralysis. Every disagreement led to a review session. Leila replayed Micah's words over and over, searching for hidden meanings. Meanwhile, Micah did the same—overanalyzing his tone, wondering if he had upset her beyond repair.

And let's not forget about the "Should we go?" dilemma. This made the process of making plans a nightmare. Neither of them could commit to a decision without overthinking the logistics, the potential outcomes, or whether the other person really wanted to go.

Their relationship was littered with unnecessary jealousy. If Micah seemed quiet after a night out with friends, Leila worried that someone had said something about her or that he was annoyed with her. Meanwhile, Micah assumed Leila's silence meant she was upset with him, when in fact, he was just thinking about what to make for dinner the next day.

Their overthinking habits had become an invisible third party in their relationship. It wasn't them against the problem—it was them against each other.

One night, after a particularly ridiculous argument (over whether Leila's "I'm fine" actually meant fine or secretly furious), they sat on the couch, exhausted. Micah rubbed his temples.

"I'm not going to assume what you meant by that," she said. "I'll just ask you instead."

Micah blinked. *Was that... an option?*

She smiled. "I don't have to figure out every single thing in my head. I can just be here."

Micah's Strategy: Nature Walks for a Mental Reset

Micah had always loved the outdoors, so he started taking more solo hikes. Fresh air, the sound of leaves crunching beneath his feet—it all helped quiet his brain.

After a long workday, instead of replaying conversations with Leila or mentally critiquing himself, he'd lace up his boots and head outside.

One afternoon, after a particularly stressful week, he invited Leila to join him. They walked in silence for a bit before Micah finally said, "You know, not every quiet moment means something's wrong."

Leila squeezed his hand. "I know." Then came the unexpected discovery: working out together.

One Saturday morning, they signed up for a strength-training class on a whim. Halfway through, as they struggled through squats, they started cracking jokes about their shaky legs.

For once, they weren't overanalyzing or second-guessing each other. They were just in it. In the moment. Afterward, as they sat on the floor, sweaty and out of breath, Leila laughed. "I don't think I overthought anything for a whole hour."

Micah grinned. "I know, right? It's kind of nice not to be in our own heads all the time." It became their new thing—morning workouts, walks, and letting go of the need to control every thought.

How It Changed Their Marriage

And just like that, they experienced fewer assumptions and more clarity. Instead of overanalyzing each other's words, they simply asked what the other meant.

They also welcomed less anxiety and more trust. They stopped assuming the worst and started trusting their bond.

Soon, in came more fun and less pressure. Their workouts became a way to connect without words—just movement, presence, and laughter.

One night, after a long day, Leila turned to Micah. "We really are getting better at this whole... not making up problems that don't exist thing, huh?" Micah smiled, pulling her close. "Yeah. Who knew peace of mind was this much work?"

They both laughed—because for the first time in a long time, they weren't thinking too hard about it. They were just being together. And that was enough.

Overthinking doesn't go away overnight. But with the right habits—whether it's meditation, movement, or getting outside—it does get easier. And when you stop treating your thoughts like facts, you make more room for what actually matters: love, connection, and being fully present with the people who mean the most.

Could Leila and Micah's story be yours? Maybe it's time to try your version of mental freedom habits and see what changes for you.

Let's dive into this chapter, where you'll discover practical strategies to build daily habits that change your mental landscape. Whether it's integrating mindful reflection into your routine, setting up moments of self-compassion, or finding small rituals that keep your thoughts in check, each tool is designed to help you harness the power of your mind for good. Get ready to explore, experiment, and build a foundation that supports lasting peace and deeper, more fulfilling connections with yourself and those around you.

Daily Practices for Mental Clarity

Daily practices for mental clarity can change your everyday routine into a sanctuary of calm and focus. Let's explore three key strategies that can help you build mental freedom and start each day on a positive note.

Meditation for a Calmer Mind

Meditation is a powerful tool that trains your brain to observe your thoughts without getting entangled in them. Studies have shown that after only eight weeks of mindful attention meditation, the amygdala—the part of your brain that processes stress—is less reactive (Desbordes et al., 2012). Here's a simple, beginner-friendly meditation practice you can try for just 10 minutes a day:

1. **Find a quiet space:** Make sure you are comfortable in a space where you won't be disturbed and close your eyes.
2. **Focus on your breath:** Breathe slowly and deeply, paying attention to your breath as it enters and exits your body.
3. **Guided mindfulness script:** Gently remind yourself, *Not every thought is a truth—some are just noise.*
4. **Observe without judgment:** If a thought pops up, acknowledge it and let it pass, returning your focus to your breath.

Try starting your day with this small ritual, setting a calm tone that helps you handle challenges with greater clarity and emotional balance.

Nature Walks: The Power of Unplugging

Taking a walk in nature is a mental reset. When you step away from screens and daily distractions, you invite a sense of wonder and relaxation. Try turning your walks into mindful adventures:

- **Leave your phone behind:** Disconnect to reconnect with your surroundings.
- **5-4-3-2-1 grounding exercise:** During your walk, observe:
- 5 things you can see, like soft clouds or the clear sky.
- 4 things you can touch, like the rough bark of a tree or soft grass.
- 3 things you can hear, like birds chirping or leaves rustling.
- 2 things you can smell, like fresh earth or blooming flowers.
- 1 thing you can taste, perhaps a sip of water or the fresh air.

This exercise pulls you into the present moment, reducing anxious thoughts and refreshing your mind.

Exercises: Creative Flow Breaks

Engaging in creative activities can be a powerful antidote to overthinking. When you channel your thoughts into something artistic, you can shift your mental focus and nurture a sense of calm. Here are some unique ways to integrate creativity into your daily routine:

- **Doodle or sketch:** Even if you don't consider yourself an artist, taking a few minutes to doodle can be incredibly liberating. Let your hand move freely on the paper, creating shapes and lines without judgment. This playful expression can help release pent-up thoughts.
- **Write a stream of consciousness:** Set a timer for 10 minutes and write down everything that comes to mind without editing or censoring yourself. This exercise helps clear mental clutter and allows your thoughts to flow naturally, providing clarity and a fresh perspective.
- **Dance it out:** Put on your favorite music and have a solo dance party. Allow your body to move in ways that feel good, letting go of any thoughts that weigh you down. This fun movement elevates your mood and reconnects you with your body.
- **Appreciate nature:** Go outside and immerse yourself in the beauty of nature. Take a moment to observe your surroundings—listen to the rustle of leaves, feel the sunlight on your skin, or appreciate vibrant colors. This mindful practice can ground you in the present and reduce overthinking.

Remember, the goal isn't perfection; it's about enjoying the process and creating a mental space where creativity can blossom and worries fade away.

Blending these daily practices into your routine creates a foundation for mental clarity and emotional balance. Whether you're meditating, walking in nature, or engaging in physical exercise, each practice is a step that brings you closer to building habits that free your mind from overthinking, empowering you to live with more confidence and presence.

Reducing Social Media Time to Reclaim Your Mind

Social media can be a double-edged sword. It connects us with loved ones but also has the potential to pull us into an overthinking trap. When you're doom-scrolling or caught in the cycle of comparison, it's easy to start second-guessing your decisions and feeling self-doubt, especially in your relationships. You might even feel like there's an invisible audience scrutinizing your every move, which only amplifies your worries and insecurities.

Here are some practical digital detox strategies to help reclaim your mind:

- **Set phone-free zones and designated screen times:** Create specific areas in your home—like your bedroom or dining area—where devices are off-limits. Try scheduling periods during the day when you intentionally disconnect, allowing your mind to reset and focus on the moment.
- **Use app blockers and grayscale mode:** Install app blockers that limit your access to social media during key times to reduce the allure of endless scrolling. Switching your phone display to grayscale can also make it less visually stimulating and addictive.
- **Replace scrolling with an offline habit:** Find an alternative that nourishes you—whether it's reading a book, journaling your thoughts, or engaging in a face-to-face conversation. These offline activities not only divert your attention but also enrich your daily experiences and

relationships.

By incorporating these strategies, you can diminish the hold that social media has on your mind, freeing up space for more positive and authentic connections. Reducing your social media time isn't about cutting yourself off completely; it's about reclaiming your mental space so that your thoughts— and your relationships—can flourish without the weight of constant comparison and self-doubt.

Decision-Making Routines to Reduce Mental Load

Every day, you're bombarded with choices—from deciding what to eat for breakfast to choosing the outfit that best fits your mood. This constant stream of decisions can lead to the dreaded decision fatigue. We've chatted about how this happens when your brain gets exhausted from endlessly weighing options. When you're tired from decision-making, it's all too easy for overthinking to take the wheel, leaving you stressed and mentally drained.

Here are some strategies to reduce your mental load by automating the smaller choices:

- **Automate small daily decisions:** Creating a default mode for everyday choices can free up precious mental space. For instance, consider Emily, who plans her meals and outfits for the week in advance. By reducing the number of choices she makes daily, Emily conserves her energy for decisions that truly matter.

- **Embrace "good enough" decision-making:** Perfectionism can be a real trap. Instead of agonizing over every detail, give yourself permission to choose what's good enough. Imagine you're picking a restaurant for dinner—rather than spending hours comparing every option, trust your gut and select the one that sounds appealing. This approach not only cuts down on overthinking but also reduces stress.
- **Use faster decision-making strategies**
- **Gut-checking:** Trust your first instinct. Often, your initial reaction is a solid guide, saving you from overanalyzing every option.
- **Set time limits:** Challenge yourself to make decisions quickly. For example, give yourself just 30 seconds to decide what to have for lunch. With practice, you'll notice that not every decision requires deep deliberation.

When you streamline your daily decisions, you can reduce decision fatigue and, in turn, diminish the overthinking loop. Every small choice you automate brings you closer to a clearer, more relaxed mind—leaving you more time and energy for the things that truly matter in your life and relationships.

Creating Boundaries With Your Thoughts

Creating boundaries with your thoughts is all about learning to observe without absorbing. You have the ability to notice your mental chatter without getting caught up in every word. Here's how you can start creating that mental space:

- **Learning to observe without absorbing:** Instead of clinging to every worry or self-criticism, simply observe them. For example, when Amy feels overwhelmed by self-doubt, she takes a step back, notices the thought, and reminds herself that it's just a temporary visitor—not a defining truth.

- **The "Emotion Indicator" exercise:** Attach physical sensations or body movements to your emotions. For example, when you feel anxious, clench your fists; when you feel calm, take deep breaths and relax your shoulders. By becoming aware of the physical manifestations of your emotions, you can learn to separate them from your thoughts, creating a clearer perspective on what you're experiencing in the moment.

- **The "Cloud in the Sky" technique:** When a negative thought arises, picture it as a bubble floating past you instead of weighing you down. This visualization helps you see that your thoughts are transient, allowing you to detach from them and focus on what truly matters.

- **The thought jar method:** Visualize your thoughts as colorful pebbles, each representing a different emotion or concern. When a troubling thought arises, imagine placing it in a jar on a shelf. This acts as a mental storage space where you can revisit the thought later without letting it consume your present moment. This strategy helps create a sense of distance and control over your mental clutter.

- **Separating emotions from facts in relationships:** Emotions can color our perceptions of events. When John feels hurt after a misunderstanding, he takes a moment to ask himself, *What are the facts here?* By distinguishing between the raw emotion and the actual situation, he finds it easier to address problems without overreacting.

- **The "Thought Traffic Light" technique:** Picture your thoughts as vehicles on a busy road. When you notice a negative thought, visualize it as a red light stopping it in its tracks. Allow it to sit there while you focus on the green light thoughts—those that uplift and motivate you. This exercise encourages you to prioritize positive and constructive thoughts over negative ones.

- **Naming the inner critic:** One effective way to create distance from negative thoughts is to give your inner critic a name. Sophie's inner voice is constantly saying, *You're not enough.* She playfully names it "Worry Wendy." This simple act of personification can strip the thought of its power, making it easier to dismiss those harmful messages.

- **The *Is This Helpful?* question:** When a thought begins to spiral, pause and ask yourself, *Is this thought really helping me right now?* This quick mental check can filter out thoughts that lead to unnecessary stress and redirect your focus toward more constructive perspectives.

When you practice these techniques, you're not trying to eliminate your thoughts but rather to build a healthy boundary between you and the constant stream of inner dialogue. This way, you empower yourself to choose which thoughts to engage with, paving the way for clearer thinking and more balanced relationships.

Action Plan for Mental Freedom

This is your roadmap to reclaiming mental freedom. It's designed to help you break free from overthinking by identifying your triggers, incorporating daily clarity habits, and setting practical boundaries.

1. **Identify your triggers:** Start by noticing what sets off your overthinking. Is it a particular conversation, a stressful work situation, or even scrolling through social media? For example, you might find that checking your notifications first thing in the morning sends you spiraling into self-doubt. Recognizing these triggers is the first step in regaining control.

2. **Choose two daily mental clarity habits:** Pick two practices that resonate with you and can easily fit into your day. This might be a 10-minute meditation to calm your mind or a refreshing nature walk that grounds you in the present. Whether you decide on journaling to clear your thoughts or engaging in a quick exercise session, these habits are your daily anchors for mental clarity.

3. **Implement one social media detox strategy:** Make a conscious effort to reclaim your time and mental space from social media. Try limiting your usage, unfollow accounts that trigger comparison, or schedule designated screen-free breaks. For instance, you might choose to set your phone to grayscale or create a phone-free zone during meals.

4. **Automate three small decisions in your day:** Reduce decision fatigue by streamlining routine choices. Automate

your daily decisions by planning meals ahead, simplifying your wardrobe, or setting a fixed morning routine. When you let go of the little choices that don't truly matter, you free up mental energy for what's most important.

5. **Use a mental boundaries technique when overthinking starts:** When you catch yourself slipping into overthinking, deploy a boundary-setting tool. Try the "bubbles in the sky" visualization, or ask yourself, *Is this thought really helpful?* This quick mental check helps you detach from unproductive worries and refocus on the present.

Following this action plan sets you up to actively build a more resilient, clear, and balanced mindset. Each step is a commitment to giving yourself permission to simplify, reset, and, ultimately, achieve greater mental freedom.

Final Thoughts

As we wrap up this chapter, take a moment to appreciate the tools and strategies you've added to your mental freedom kit. You've learned how to spot your triggers, create daily habits for clarity, cut down on social media noise, simplify everyday decisions, and even set healthy boundaries with your thoughts. Each of these steps is a powerful move away from the overthinking that fuels anxiety, indecision, and relationship struggles.

Now, imagine the possibilities when you shift your mindset from being overwhelmed by every little worry to establishing a growth mindset. This mindset helps you build resilience, adapt to life's challenges, and develop emotional intelligence— qualities that can transform your relationships and overall well-being.

In our next chapter, we'll explore how to make that shift, guiding you toward a way of thinking that acknowledges challenges and uses them to build a richer, more fulfilling life.

8

Chapter 8: From Overthinking to Growth Mindset

Macy stared at the calendar, a familiar mix of frustration and exhaustion washing over her. Two years. That's how long she'd been engaged to Josh. Two years of excitement, love, and... decision fatigue. They should have been married by now—if it were up to her, they would have been. But every major decision had been postponed, debated, or completely abandoned in the name of overthinking.

At first, it was kind of endearing. Josh wanted everything to be perfect. That was sweet, right? But then it became a pattern.

Should we invite my second cousin's ex-wife? What if people hate the food? Will summer be too hot? Will winter be too cold?

Each time, before Macy could blink, six more months had passed. The wedding date— a moving target. Josh wasn't just indecisive. He was stuck. Completely paralyzed by the what-ifs, unable to commit to anything that wasn't absolutely foolproof.

One night, after yet another discussion that ended in circles, Macy finally said, "We need help." Josh agreed. Soon, he found himself sitting across from a therapist who listened carefully before sliding a small notebook across the table.

"This is your 'what-if journal,'" the therapist explained. "Every time you catch yourself overthinking a decision, I want you to write down the top three 'what-ifs' holding you back. Then, right next to each one, list any actual evidence that supports those fears."

Josh raised an eyebrow. "And then what?"

"Then, I want you to rewrite those what-ifs, but in a positive way."

Josh sighed, but he tried it. And wouldn't you know it, his first real test came the very next day.

For the first time in forever, Josh started seeing that his brain had been working against him. He wasn't searching for the right decision—he was searching for certainty. And in real life, certainty doesn't exist.

As he kept journaling, Josh slowly began making choices without spiraling into a panic. He wasn't perfect, but he was trying. And for Macy, that meant the world. Because for the first time in two years, she finally felt like she could mark something on that calendar.

The wedding? It was happening.

In this chapter, we'll explore how shifting from that relentless loop of doubts to a growth mindset can change everything—transforming challenges into building blocks and fostering resilience, adaptability, and emotional intelligence. Imagine turning those moments of hesitation into opportunities for learning and self-improvement, where every setback becomes a chance to grow stronger and build deeper, more fulfilling connections.

Fixed Mindset vs. Growth Mindset: Spotting the Differences

Understanding how we view our relationships can make a huge difference in our overall well-being. Sometimes, our minds are quick to jump to negative conclusions that can cause unnecessary stress and conflict. To help you pinpoint whether your thoughts lean toward a fixed mindset or a growth mindset, I've put together a comparison chart.

This chart highlights common scenarios in relationships and contrasts the fixed mindset's immediate negative assumptions with the more compassionate, open, and adaptable responses of a growth mindset. Use this as a guide to reflect on your own thinking patterns and explore ways to create more resilient and fulfilling connections.

This chart highlights how a fixed mindset can lead to quick, negative assumptions, while a growth mindset opens up more adaptive and compassionate ways of thinking that not only nurture your own well-being but also strengthen your relationships.

Overthinkers Stuck in a Fear of Failure

When we overthink, we often find ourselves trapped in a fixed mindset, where self-criticism, perfectionism, and fear of failure create a loop that holds us back from accepting change and growth.

For instance, when you make a small mistake—say, misspeaking during a conversation—you might immediately think, *I'm so stupid,* instead of recognizing that everyone slips up sometimes. This harsh self-criticism convinces you that your abilities are static, preventing you from learning from your errors.

Perfectionism plays a big role, too. Imagine you're working on a personal project and every detail must be flawless before you share it with others. The pressure to meet an impossible standard can lead to procrastination or even complete avoidance of the project, as the idea of anything less than perfect feels unacceptable. This leaves you stuck, never giving yourself the opportunity to grow through trial and error.

Then, there's the fear of failure. You might hesitate to try new experiences—like applying for that dream job or asking someone out—because you're convinced that failure would confirm your worst self-doubts. Overthinking these scenarios intensifies your anxiety, making it easier to settle into a fixed mindset rather than taking a chance on personal growth.

Recognizing these patterns is the first step toward shifting into a mindset that celebrates learning, resilience, and continuous improvement.

Consider the story of Ashley. In her early relationships, Ashley was often overwhelmed by overthinking. She would instantly assume that a delayed text meant her partner didn't care, spiraling into self-criticism and even perfectionism about being the perfect partner. For instance, after a minor disagreement, she felt convinced that her every flaw had been exposed and that the relationship was doomed. This fear of failure made her hesitant to address issues directly, trapping her in a cycle of negative assumptions.

Over time, with the support of a close friend and some honest self-reflection, Ashley began to notice these fixed mindset patterns. Instead of immediately jumping to conclusions, she started to consider alternative explanations, acknowledging that perhaps her partner was simply busy or stressed.

Reframing her thoughts and viewing each challenge as an opportunity allowed her to learn and grow. Ashley gradually embraced a growth mindset. This shift not only eased her anxiety but also allowed her to communicate more openly and build a deeper, more resilient connection with her partner.

The Mindset Shift Test

You can use this test to assess your thought patterns and practice small, powerful adjustments. Each step is designed to help you notice automatic, fixed-mindset reactions and reframe them with a growth-oriented perspective. Follow these steps:

Identify the trigger and your automatic thought:

- **Exercise:** Think of a recent moment when you felt anxious or upset in a relationship. Write down the situation and your immediate thought.
- **Example:** You notice your partner didn't text back quickly. Your initial thought might be, *They must not care about me.*

Examine the evidence:

- **Exercise:** Ask yourself: *What facts do I have? Is there evidence to support this thought, or might I be making an assumption?*
- **Example:** Consider that your partner has a busy day at work. Their delay might have nothing to do with their feelings for you.

Consider alternative explanations:

- **Exercise:** List at least two other possible reasons for the situation. This broadens your perspective beyond the initial negative thought.
- **Example:** *Maybe they're caught up in a meeting* or *They might have a distraction right now.*

Reframe the thought:

- **Exercise:** Transform your original thought into one that reflects a growth mindset by incorporating the alternative explanations.
- **Example:** Replace *They must not care* with *Perhaps they're busy; I can use this time to focus on something I enjoy.*

Reflect on the impact:

- **Exercise:** Notice how this slight shift in perspective makes you feel. Does it ease your anxiety? Does it open up new ways to approach your relationship?
- **Example:** You might find that acknowledging alternative reasons reduces your worry and helps you communicate more effectively later.

Why Small Shifts Matter

Even micro-adjustments like these can rewire your thought patterns over time. Each time you pause and challenge an automatic, fixed mindset response, you're training your brain to consider more balanced, compassionate, and realistic viewpoints. Think of it like building mental resilience—each small shift is a step toward a healthier, more adaptable mindset that benefits both your inner world and your relationships.

Real-World Application Techniques

Integrating a growth mindset into your everyday life might feel challenging at first, but it all starts with small, practical steps.

Here are some real-world application techniques, complete with tangible examples and actionable tips, to help you turn everyday challenges into opportunities for growth.

Identifying Opportunities for Growth

Here's a list of strategies to help you identify opportunities for growth in both personal and professional aspects of your life:

- **Recognize daily challenges as learning moments:** Every time you face a setback—like a work project that didn't go as planned or a misunderstanding with a friend—you have a chance to learn. For example, if a presentation at work falls flat, instead of thinking, *I'm terrible at public speaking*, try asking, *What can I do differently next time?*
- **Embrace feedback:** When your partner or colleague offers feedback, see it as a tool for improvement. For instance, if a friend tells you that you sometimes interrupt during conversations, consider this an opportunity to work on your listening skills rather than a personal flaw.
- **View failures as growth:** Think about a time you attempted something new—like trying to learn a new recipe or sport—and it didn't work out perfectly. Instead of giving up, use that experience to adjust your approach. Every failure provides valuable insights that pave the way for future success.

Setting Realistic Goals

Setting realistic goals is crucial for achieving success and staying motivated. Here's a helpful list to guide you in establishing effective and attainable objectives that will lead you toward your dreams:

- **Create specific, measurable goals:** Instead of setting vague goals like "I want to be healthier," set a target such as "I will walk 30 minutes every day this week." This makes your progress trackable and your ambitions more achievable.
- **Break down larger ambitions:** If you're dreaming of running a marathon, start with a plan to run a 5K, then gradually increase your distance. Each small milestone builds confidence and momentum toward your larger goal.
- **Celebrate wins:** Recognize and celebrate every small achievement. For example, if you manage to stick to your daily writing goal, reward yourself with a favorite treat or a break doing something you love. These celebrations reinforce your progress and motivate you to keep going.

Creating a Supportive Environment

Here are some ways to foster this uplifting atmosphere and actively engage with those who inspire and motivate you:

- **Surround yourself with positive influences:** Engage with friends, colleagues, or online communities that champion growth and learning. Join groups or forums where people share their progress and challenges, such as a local meetup for personal development or a professional mastermind group.

· **Avoid negative influences:** Be mindful of relationships or environments that drain your energy or reinforce negative self-talk. Instead, seek out mentors or role models who inspire you with their growth stories and practical advice.

· **Utilize mentors or role models:** Connect with someone who has navigated similar challenges. For example, if you're trying to shift your career, a mentor who's experienced a similar journey can provide insights, encouragement, and practical tips on overcoming obstacles.

Practicing Self-Compassion

Here are some key practices to help you become kinder to yourself, embrace growth, and view setbacks as essential steps:

· **Be kind to yourself:** When setbacks occur, practice self-compassion. Instead of harsh self-criticism, acknowledge your struggles without judgment. For example, if you miss a deadline, reflect on what factors contributed to it and what you can adjust next time, rather than berating yourself.

· **Understand that growth is a process:** Remember that personal development is full of ups and downs. Treat negative experiences as platforms for learning. Each misstep is simply a part of the process, not a reflection of your worth.

· **Turn negative experiences into learning opportunities:**

153

Use journaling or self-reflection to capture lessons from challenging moments. For instance, after a disagreement with a friend, write down what you learned about communication and how you might approach similar situations more effectively in the future.

When you apply these real-world techniques, you'll start to see that every challenge is a lesson toward a stronger, more resilient you. Each minor adjustment builds a foundation for a more adaptable mindset, changing everyday obstacles into valuable opportunities for growth.

Reframing Challenges: How to Shift Your Mental Framework

Here are four hands-on exercises to help you reframe challenges and shift your mental framework. Each exercise is designed to challenge overthinking patterns and replace them with more constructive, growth-focused thoughts.

Exercise 1: The "What If..." Reframe

Objective: Turn negative "what if" scenarios into opportunities for growth.

1. **Identify a negative thought:** Think of a recent moment when you overthought a situation. For example, if you thought, *What if they get annoyed when I express my feelings?* write it down.

2. **Create a positive alternative:** Next, reframe that thought using a growth perspective: *What if I learn something valuable by expressing myself?*
3. **Compare and reflect:** Write both versions side by side. Reflect on how each thought makes you feel. Which perspective opens up more possibilities for growth?

Exercise 2: Perspective-Taking Challenge

Objective: Improve your interactions by considering alternative viewpoints.

1. **Recall a recent interaction:** Choose a recent conflict or miscommunication (e.g., a conversation that left you feeling frustrated).
2. **Document your view:** Write down your initial perspective and feelings about the situation.
3. **Adopt another perspective:** Now, put yourself in the other person's shoes. Ask: *What might they have been feeling or experiencing?* Write down at least two alternative explanations.
4. **Reflect on the differences:** Compare both viewpoints and note how this shift could change your reaction or communication in future interactions.

Exercise 3: The "Failure Is Feedback" Method

Objective: Transform perceived failures into learning opportunities.

1. **Select a "failure" moment:** Think of a recent instance where you felt you failed, for example, a conversation that didn't go as planned.
2. **Write down your immediate reaction:** Document your initial thought, such as *I failed at this conversation.*
3. **Extract the feedback:** Reflect on what you can learn from the situation. Write down at least one lesson or actionable insight, like noticing that you rushed your words under stress.
4. **Plan for future success:** Note a specific strategy you can apply next time, reinforcing that every setback is simply feedback for growth.

Exercise 4: Self-Talk Rewriting

Objective: Replace negative self-talk with growth-focused alternatives.

1. **Identify negative self-talk:** Notice a recurring negative phrase you tell yourself (e.g., *I always mess up when I try to express my needs*).
2. **Document the thought:** Write down the negative thought as it appears in your mind.
3. **Reframe the thought:** Change it into a growth-oriented statement. For instance, change it to, *Every time I share my needs, I learn how to communicate better.*
4. **Repetition and reinforcement:** Whenever you catch yourself engaging in negative self-talk, refer back to your rewritten statement. Over time, this practice will help build a more compassionate inner dialogue.

When you regularly practice these exercises, you'll gradually rewire your thought patterns and continue to grow. Each shift helps you move toward a more resilient mindset, fostering better relationships and a healthier self-view.

Action Plan: Implement Growth Mindset Practices

Below is an actionable plan to help you integrate a growth mindset into your daily life and relationships. This step-by-step guide includes exercises, challenges, and strategies to ensure that you can track your progress, celebrate wins, and practice self-kindness even when setbacks occur.

Personal Reflection Exercise

Objective: Identify one recurring overthinking pattern and reframe it into a growth-focused thought.

1. Choose a recurring overthinking pattern. For instance, if you often think, *They must not care if they don't reply immediately,* note it down.
2. Write down the negative thought and then brainstorm a growth-oriented alternative. For example, reframe it to, *They might be busy, and this is a chance for me to focus on something I enjoy.*
3. Reflect on how this reframing changes your emotional response. Journaling your thoughts can help you track your progress over time.

The 3-Day Growth Challenge

Objective: Experiment with changing your thinking patterns over a short period.

- **Day 1: Awareness:** Throughout the day, note moments when you catch yourself overthinking. Use a small notebook or a notes app to record the situation and your initial thoughts.
- **Day 2: Reframe in real-time:** When you recognize a negative thought, pause and apply the "What If…" reframe. For example, change *What if I make a fool of myself?* to *What if I learn something valuable by trying?* Record both the original and reframed thought.
- **Day 3: Reflection and adjustment:** Review your notes from the past two days. Identify which reframing strategies worked best for you. Adjust your approach if needed, and set one personal goal for continued practice.

Setting Relationship Mindset Goals

Objective: Create specific, measurable, and attainable goals to foster a growth mindset in your relationships.

1. **Define a goal:** For example, "I will practice open communication with my partner by expressing my feelings calmly and constructively during disagreements."
2. **Track progress:** Use a daily journal or a digital tracking tool to record moments when you successfully applied

your growth mindset. Note improvements, even small ones, in your communication and emotional responses.

3. **Review regularly:** At the end of each week, evaluate your progress. Identify what worked and what needs adjustment, and celebrate your successes—no matter how small.

What to Do When You Slip Back Into Overthinking

Objective: Use self-compassion techniques to get back on track when old habits resurface.

1. **Pause and breathe:** When you notice overthinking creeping in, take a few deep breaths to regain focus.
2. **Self-kindness check-in:** Acknowledge the slip-up without harsh judgment. Remind yourself that setbacks are normal and part of the learning process.
3. **Reapply your reframe:** Look at your recorded negative thought and reframe it using the techniques from your personal reflection exercise. Write down the new thought to reinforce the shift.
4. **Reach out:** Consider discussing your challenges with a trusted friend or mentor who supports your growth journey.

Growth Mindset Mantras

Objective: Reinforce a resilient, self-aware mindset with daily reminders.

- **Examples of mantras:**
- "Every challenge is an opportunity to learn and grow."
- "I am capable of overcoming obstacles with grace."
- "My mistakes are stepping stones to my success."
- **Daily practice:** Choose one or two mantras that resonate with you and write them on a sticky note, phone wallpaper, or journal page. Repeat these phrases each morning or whenever you feel overwhelmed.

By following this action plan, you'll take tangible steps to shift your mental framework. Each exercise and strategy is designed to help you build resilience, foster healthier relationships, and ultimately rewire your thought patterns from overthinking to a growth-focused mindset. Remember, progress is a journey of small, consistent adjustments—celebrate each step along the way.

Final Thoughts

As we wrap up this chapter on shifting from overthinking to a growth mindset, take a moment to appreciate the small victories you've made. You've learned to catch those spiraling thoughts and reframe them with techniques like the "What If..." exercise, perspective-taking challenges, and even turning failures into feedback.

In the next chapter, we're going to explore the social side of overthinking—delving into how our internal dialogues impact our friendships, work relationships, and community connections. We'll uncover practical strategies to manage social anxiety, build stronger bonds, and truly thrive in your interactions with others. Get ready to expand your growth mindset into your social world.

9

Chapter 9: The Social Side of Overthinking

Jason was, by all accounts, a catch. His friends told him so. His coworkers told him so. Even his mom, who was generally stingy with compliments, said, "Jason, any woman would be lucky to have you." And yet, despite his ability to meet people with ease—he was friendly, kind, and had a great sense of humor— his dating life was an absolute mess.

It wasn't the first impression that got him. No, Jason could confidently say, "Hi, my name is Jason," without breaking a sweat. But after that? That's where things started to unravel.

As soon as the conversation moved past introductions, Jason's brain went into full-blown panic mode.

Did that joke land?

Do I sound intelligent, or do I sound like I barely graduated high school?

Should I be funny? Thoughtful? Oh god, am I rambling?

Before he knew it, he wasn't having a conversation anymore—he was performing. He adjusted himself based on what he thought the other person wanted. If they seemed serious, he'd lean into being deep and intellectual. If they laughed at something, he'd keep the jokes rolling even if he had a story he actually wanted to tell. Somewhere along the way, his real personality got lost in translation.

It wasn't until a date with a woman named Rebecca that Jason truly saw how bad it had gotten. Rebecca was cool. Like, really cool. Smart, funny, easy to talk to—except Jason wasn't actually talking, he was just saying things he thought she'd like. She mentioned she loved hiking, so suddenly, Jason was a passionate hiker (he wasn't). She talked about obscure indie movies, so Jason pretended to be an expert in all things cinema (he wasn't).

But then, halfway through dinner, Rebecca tilted her head and asked, "So, what are you actually into?" Jason froze.

What am I actually into? He blanked. Not because he didn't have interests but because he had spent the last hour making sure he was the kind of guy she'd want, not being himself.

That night, instead of rewatching the date in his head on an endless loop, picking apart everything he said, Jason sat with one single realization: He was exhausted from trying so hard.

If he wanted to find someone he could truly connect with, he had to be himself. To do that, he had to stop overanalyzing every single interaction like it was a test he could pass or fail.

The next time he went on a date, Jason did something radical.

Instead of planning what he was going to say or crafting a "charming" personality to fit the other person, he focused on just talking. If he wanted to make a joke, he did. If he had an opinion on something, he shared it—even if he wasn't sure it was the "right" one.

And when his brain tried to spiral into post-date analysis, he reminded himself of one thing: His goal wasn't to impress someone—it was to connect.

Slowly but surely, Jason started catching himself when he fell into the old habit of performance mode. He started pausing before responding, giving himself a second to check in: *Am I saying this because it's true or because I think it's what they want to hear?*

He still had moments of doubt, but instead of getting stuck in them, he gently reminded himself: *I am safe to speak my truth.*

And when he finally met someone who liked him for him—not some curated version of himself—it felt like a breath of fresh air. Overthinking was never the problem; Jason just had to learn to trust himself enough to stop performing and start showing up as his real, unfiltered self. And that? That was where real connection began.

Overthinking has a sneaky way of turning even the simplest social interactions into a full-blown mental obstacle course. You replay conversations, dissect every text message, and convince yourself that your friends secretly hate you just because they took a little too long to respond. Sound familiar?

Overthinking in relationships—whether with friends, family, or romantic partners—can lead to social anxiety, people-pleasing, and communication struggles that make connecting feel exhausting instead of energizing. But you don't have to stay stuck in analysis paralysis. In this chapter, we'll explore how overthinking affects your relationships and, more importantly, how to quiet the mental noise so you can show up with confidence, ease, and authenticity. Let's get you out of your head and back into meaningful, real-life connections.

Managing Social Anxiety

Overthinking and social anxiety go hand in hand, especially in intimate relationships where vulnerability is at play. When you care deeply about someone, the stakes feel higher—so you analyze, overanalyze, and then analyze some more.

Did I say the wrong thing?

Should I have texted back sooner?

Why did they pause before answering?

This mental loop can make relationships feel more like a test you're destined to fail rather than a connection to enjoy. Let's break that cycle so you can show up with confidence and ease.

The Social Spiral: How Overthinking Fuels Anxiety

Meet Taylor. Taylor has been dating Adam for six months, and things are going well, at least on the surface. But inside, Taylor is constantly overthinking. When Adam doesn't respond to a text for a few hours, Taylor assumes he's losing interest. When Adam shares a story about an ex, Taylor mentally dissects every word, searching for hidden meaning. Even after a great date, Taylor replays every conversation, wondering if they talked too much, not enough, or said something weird without realizing it. This anxious loop makes Taylor feel more distant from Adam, even though nothing has happened. Can you relate?

This is the overthinking–anxiety spiral in action:

1. **Before a social interaction:** You anticipate every possible way it could go wrong.
2. **During the interaction:** You monitor yourself so closely that you struggle to be present.
3. **After the interaction:** You replay it, looking for mistakes and judging yourself harshly.

This cycle keeps you from experiencing real connection. I'm here to show you how to rewire your thinking.

Reframing Your Thoughts: From Self-Doubt to Self-Trust

The key to breaking free is shifting from self-criticism to curiosity. Instead of assuming the worst, start asking yourself better questions:

- Instead of *Did I sound stupid?* try *What's one thing I enjoyed about that conversation?*
- Instead of *Are they mad at me?* try *What evidence do I have that they're upset?*
- Instead of *What if they leave me?* try *How can I focus on enjoying the present moment with them?*

Let's go back to Taylor. One night, Adam is quiet and doesn't text goodnight. Taylor's first instinct? Panic. *Did I say something wrong? Are they pulling away?* But instead of spiraling, Taylor pauses and asks, *Could Adam just be busy with something else?* The moment Taylor shifts from fear to curiosity, the anxiety loses its grip. Later, Adam mentions having a stressful day at work—confirming that Taylor's initial panic was unnecessary. This is how you build self-trust: by noticing when overthinking takes over and gently steering your thoughts in a more balanced direction.

Quick Grounding Techniques for Social Situations

When social anxiety hits, you need tools that work fast. Here are a few unconventional tricks:

- **Sip and breathe:** Take a drink of cold water and inhale deeply through your nose while swallowing. The slow, deliberate movement calms your nervous system instantly.
- **Mindful micro-movement:** If your anxiety spikes mid-conversation, shift your weight from one foot to the other

or roll your shoulders back. It tricks your brain into feeling more at ease.

- **Hum:** Yep, it's true. If you hum (or even sing a little tune), it stimulates your vagus nerve and immediately grounds you, reducing stress and anxiety (Laderer, 2024).

Shifting Focus: From Overthinking to Connection

One of the best ways to ease social anxiety is to shift your focus away from yourself and onto *the* interaction itself.

Try this:

- Be genuinely curious about your partner's thoughts. Instead of worrying about what you just said, ask them a follow-up question.
- Listen for emotions rather than words. Instead of analyzing the exact phrasing of what they said, notice the tone and energy behind it.
- Play a mental game: Pretend you're a journalist and your goal is to uncover something interesting about them. This shifts your focus to learning rather than performing.

Overthinking in relationships doesn't mean you're doomed— it just means you care. But caring shouldn't come at the cost of your peace of mind. With practice, you can quiet the mental noise, trust yourself, and experience the connection you deserve—without fear running the show.

People-Pleasing Tendencies: Breaking Free from the Approval Trap

People-pleasing is sneaky. It feels like kindness, like being a good partner, like keeping the peace. But in reality, it's overthinking in disguise. When you're constantly anticipating your partner's needs, filtering your words to avoid conflict, or saying yes when you desperately want to say no, you're not strengthening the relationship—you're shrinking yourself to fit into it. And that's exhausting. Let's break the cycle so you can prioritize your own needs while still showing up with love and kindness.

Why We Overthink Pleasing Others And How to Stop

If you struggle with people-pleasing, it's not because you love doing things for others—it's because you're afraid of what might happen if you don't. That fear can take different forms:

- **Fear of rejection:** *If I say no, they'll think I'm selfish and stop loving me.*
- **Fear of conflict:** *If I speak up, we'll argue, and I can't handle that stress.*
- **Need for validation:** *If I do everything right, they'll see my worth and choose me.*

Recognizing why you people-please is the first step to breaking the habit. Because saying yes all the time isn't making your relationship stronger—it's making it imbalanced.

Take Wendy, for example. She's been dating Ken for a year and always goes along with what he wants. If he asks where they should eat, she says, "Wherever you want!" If he's upset, she rushes to fix it—even when she's exhausted. When she does have an opinion, she keeps it to herself because she doesn't want to "rock the boat." At first, Ken thought Wendy was just easygoing. But lately, something feels... off. She seems distant, stressed, and less affectionate.

That's the hidden cost of people-pleasing: You think you're making your partner happy, but in reality, you're slowly building resentment, disconnecting from yourself, and creating a relationship where your needs don't matter.

Recognizing People-Pleasing Behaviors

If you're wondering whether you fall into the people-pleasing trap, ask yourself:

- *Do I say yes when I really want to say no?*
- *Do I avoid speaking up about my feelings or needs to keep the peace?*
- *Do I feel responsible for my partner's emotions?*
- *Do I feel guilty when I prioritize myself?*
- *Do I overanalyze my words and actions to make sure I didn't "mess up"?*

If you answered yes to most of these, you might be stuck in the people-pleasing cycle. Here are some common scenarios where it shows up:

Scenario 1—Always agreeing:

- Before: "Sure, whatever you want is fine!" (Even when it's not.)
- After: "I'd actually love to do what you want today. Let's do that!"

Scenario 2—Avoiding difficult conversations:

- Before: "It's not a big deal; I'll just let it go." (Even though it *is* a big deal.)
- After: "Hey, this is something that's been on my mind. Can we talk about it?"

Scenario 3—Feeling responsible for their mood:

- Before: "They seem upset. What did *I* do wrong?"
- After: "They're having a tough day. I'll check in, but their emotions aren't mine to fix."

Scenario 4—Overcommitting to keep them happy:

- Before: "Of course I'll help with that! No, I don't mind at all!" (Even though you *do* mind.)
- After: "I'd love to help, but I can't this time. Maybe next time?"

Shifting From People-Pleasing to Healthy Boundaries

People-pleasing isn't love—it's self-abandonment in disguise. But you don't have to choose between your needs and your *partner's* happiness. You can have both.

Here's how:

- **Pause before saying yes:** Ask yourself: *Do I actually want to do this?* If the answer is no, practice saying, "Let me get back to you on that."
- **Start small:** If setting boundaries feels overwhelming, start with low-stakes situations, like picking a restaurant or expressing a small opinion.
- **Let go of guilt:** Prioritizing yourself doesn't mean you're selfish—it means you're human.
- **Trust that the right people will stay:** If someone truly loves and respects you, they *want* to know the real you—not just the version that always says yes.

Saying yes to everything won't make someone love you more—it'll just make you disappear. The best relationships aren't built on keeping the peace at all costs. They're built on mutual honesty, respect, and the ability to show up as your whole self. So the next time you feel the urge to overthink, pause. Breathe. And remind yourself: You are allowed to take up space in your own life.

The Difference Between Being Kind and Being a Doormat

Let's clear something up: Being kind does not mean being a doormat. Kindness is a choice—something you give freely because it aligns with your values. Being a doormat, on the other hand, is when you feel obligated to say yes, even when it drains you. It's kindness hijacked by anxiety, guilt, and the fear of disappointing others.

If you've ever thought, *Why do I always feel exhausted from giving so much?* or *Why do people take advantage of me?* It's time to check in with your motivation.

How to Tell if Your Kindness Is Authentic or Fueled by Anxiety

Ask yourself these questions the next time you say yes to something:

If your kindness is fueled by anxiety instead of genuine care, it's time to practice a powerful skill: saying no.

Rewiring Your Responses: Practicing the Power of No

Saying no shouldn't be veiled as selfishness because it is, in fact, a form of self-respect. And the best part? You can set boundaries without guilt.

Emma is the friend everyone calls when they need a favor. Rides to the airport? Done. Last-minute pet-sitting? Of course. Covering a coworker's shift again? She wants to say no, but the guilt kicks in, so she sighs and says, "Sure, I guess."

One day, Emma's boyfriend, Brandon, asked for a favor. He needed her to help him with a work project on the same night she had plans to rest and recharge. She felt torn—helping him would be nice, but she was exhausted.

Usually, she'd say yes automatically. But this time, she tried something new: pausing before answering.

She took a breath and asked herself: *Do I actually have the time and energy for this?*

The answer was no.

So, instead of her usual automatic yes, she said: "I'd love to help, but I really need a night to rest. Maybe another time?"

To her surprise, Brandon didn't get upset. He actually respected her honesty.

This slight shift—pausing before answering—helped Emma break the habit of saying yes out of obligation.

Simple Ways to Set Boundaries Without Guilt

Here's how you can start practicing the power of no today:

Use the pause rule:

- Before saying yes, take five seconds to check in with yourself. If the thought of saying yes makes you tense up, that's a sign to rethink it.

Have a "Go-To No" response:

- Keep a simple, non-apologetic response ready. Some examples:
- "I'd love to, but I can't right now."
- "I don't have the bandwidth for that, but I hope you find help!"
- "That doesn't work for me, but thanks for asking!"

Offer alternatives if you want to:

- If you genuinely want to help but can't do it their way, suggest a compromise:
- "I can't do that tonight, but I'd be happy to help next weekend."

Let go of the fear of disappointing people:

- Saying no doesn't make you mean or unkind. It just means you respect your own needs, too. The right people will understand.

Being a good partner, friend, or coworker doesn't mean bending over backward to make everyone happy. It means showing up as your full self, with honesty and self-respect. You can be kind and set boundaries. You can be generous and say no. And the more you practice this, the more you'll realize that the people who genuinely care about you don't need you to *please* them—they just need you to be you.

Healthy Boundaries—The Key to Inner Peace

Boundaries act like a mental filter, protecting your energy and helping you stop the endless cycle of analyzing every interaction. They're guardrails that keep relationships healthy and balanced. The irony? Many overthinkers resist setting boundaries because they're afraid of upsetting others—when in reality, clear boundaries actually strengthen relationships by building honesty, trust, and respect.

Let's break it down and make boundary-setting feel doable—without the guilt, stress, or overanalysis.

Setting Healthy Boundaries

Olivia is in a loving relationship with James, but she constantly feels drained. He calls her the second he has a bad day, venting for hours while she listens, comforts, and offers advice—at the expense of her own peace. She doesn't mind being supportive, but lately, she dreads the phone ringing. She tells herself, *I should be there for him*—but deep down, she resents always being the emotional sponge.

One night, after a long, exhausting day, James calls. Olivia hesitates but decides to set a small boundary. Instead of immediately picking up, she texts: "Hey, I had a rough day, too.

Can we catch up tomorrow? I really want to be present when we talk, and I need to recharge tonight."

To her surprise, James responds, "Of course! Hope you get some rest."

That's the magic of boundaries. Olivia still showed care, but she protected her own energy. Instead of ruining the relationship, it made it stronger—all because she was honest about her needs.

Here are some great tips to communicate boundaries without conflict:

Use "I" statements to express your needs:

- Instead of: "You always overwhelm me with your problems."
- Try: "I really want to support you, but I need some time to recharge before we talk."

Be direct but kind:

- Instead of: "I guess I can, if you really need me to..." (resentful and unclear)
- Try: "I can't tonight, but I'd love to help another time." (clear and firm)

Acknowledge their feelings, but stand your ground:

- Instead of: "Fine, I'll do it, but I really don't want to."

- Try: "I understand this is important to you, but I need to set this limit for myself."

Recognizing Where You Need Boundaries Most

If overthinking is taking over your life, chances are you need boundaries in these areas:

- **Emotional energy:** Are you absorbing everyone else's stress? Do you feel drained after certain conversations? If so, set boundaries around how much emotional labor you take on.
- **Time and availability:** Do you feel guilty saying no? Do you cancel your own plans to accommodate others? Start protecting your time by not over-committing.
- **Personal space and privacy:** Do you feel like your boundaries are constantly being tested? Set limits on what you share, who has access to your time, and how much emotional energy you give.

So, how can you identify your personal triggers?

Ask yourself:

- *Who or what makes me feel drained, anxious, or overextended?*
- *What situations make me feel like I have no control over my time or emotions?*
- *When do I feel the most resentful?* Resentment is a major sign that a boundary needs to be set.

Scripts and Strategies for Boundary-Setting Without Overthinking

Now that you know where you need boundaries, let's talk about how to enforce them—without spiraling into guilt or second-guessing.

Here's what to say when someone pushes your limits:

If someone ignores your time boundary:

- "I love talking with you, but I can't stay on the phone for more than 20 minutes tonight."
- "I'm happy to help, but I need a heads-up next time so I can plan accordingly."

If a partner expects too much emotional labor:

- "I want to support you, but I don't have the capacity to take this on right now. Can we talk about it later when I have more energy?"
- "I care about you, but I can't be the only one managing these situations. Let's work on finding a solution together."

If someone guilt-trips you for saying no:

- "I understand that you're disappointed, but I need to set this boundary for my own well-being."
- "I hear that this is important to you, and I wish I could help, but I can't take this on right now."

Let's look at how you can hold firm when guilt or doubt creeps in:

- **Remind yourself that boundaries are healthy:** Saying no makes you human. It ensures you are clear about your limits.
- **Give yourself permission to disappoint people:** It's okay if someone isn't thrilled with your boundary. Their feelings are theirs to manage, not yours.
- **Practice small no's first:** Start with low-stakes situations like declining an invitation or asking for space to build confidence.
- **Notice how you feel when you hold a boundary:** Instead of panicking about someone's reaction, check in with yourself. Do you feel lighter? Less stressed? More in control?

Healthy boundaries are intended to create space for deeper, more authentic connections. When you stop overthinking every interaction and start honoring your needs, you'll feel lighter, freer, and more at peace—and the people who truly respect you will adjust.

Communication Without Overanalysis—Speak Your Mind With Confidence

If you've ever left a conversation only to spend the next three hours replaying everything you said, welcome to the Overthinker's Club. We tend to treat conversations like a performance—one wrong word, and the audience (aka the person we're talking to) will surely boo us off the stage.

But people aren't analyzing your every word the way you are. Most of the time, they're just enjoying the interaction or thinking about what they'll have for dinner. Learning to trust yourself in conversations will not only ease your mind—it'll help you build stronger, more genuine connections.

Let's talk about how to speak up without overthinking.

The Overthinker's Dilemma: Did I Say That Right?

Overthinkers don't just talk—we edit, analyze, and critique ourselves mid-sentence. Before we speak, we wonder: What's the perfect way to phrase this? During the conversation, we scan for reactions: *Do they look bored?* And afterward, we dissect: *Should I have said something different?*

This need to perform keeps us from actually being present in conversations. The best interactions happen when we stop trying to say the right thing and just say what's real.

Here are some tips to let go of the need to perform in

conversations:

Shift from performance mode to connection mode:

- Instead of thinking, *What should I say to impress them?* ask yourself, *How can I connect with them?*
- Conversations aren't about delivering a perfect monologue— they're about engaging with another person.

Speak before you overthink:

- If you feel yourself hesitating and mentally editing your words before speaking, challenge yourself to say the first version that comes to mind.
- You'll be surprised how often your natural thoughts are already good enough.

People remember feelings more than words:

- No one is going to remember if you slightly misspoke or phrased something imperfectly. They'll remember how they felt around you. Aim for authenticity over perfection.

Speaking Up With Clarity and Confidence

Filtering your words out of fear—of judgment, of rejection, of saying the wrong thing makes conversations exhausting. You end up shrinking yourself, agreeing when you don't want to, or staying silent when you have something to say.

So, how can you stop filtering yourself?

- **Give yourself permission to be heard:** You don't need to wait for the perfect moment to speak. Your thoughts are valid *now*.
- **Use shorter sentences:** Overthinkers tend to overexplain. Instead, say what you mean in one sentence, then stop. If they need more details, they'll ask!
- **Trust that silence isn't awkward:** Pauses in conversations aren't as weird as they feel. You don't have to fill every silence. Let them take their turn to respond.
- **If you catch yourself rambling, pause:** If you're mid-sentence and realize you're talking in circles, you can literally stop and say, "Actually, what I mean is...". No one minds; it just makes you sound more confident.

Breaking the Habit of Replaying Conversations in Your Head

Overthinkers have an unfortunate hobby: post-conversation analysis. It goes like this:

1. You leave a conversation.
2. You immediately replay everything you said.
3. You find something embarrassing or awkward even if no one else noticed.
4. You cringe and mentally punish yourself for it.

Ethan went on a date with Chloe. They had a great time, laughed a lot, and made plans to see each other again. But later that night, Ethan's brain went into overdrive:

- *Did I talk too much about my job?*
- *That one joke—was it weird? Did she laugh because it was funny or because she felt awkward?*
- *Oh no... I interrupted her once. What if she thinks I'm rude?*

By the time Ethan was done mentally spiraling, he was convinced he'd ruined everything. But the next day? Chloe texted: "Had so much fun last night! Can't wait to see you again."

Moral of the story? The conversation you're obsessing over is not as deep in the other person's mind as it is in yours.

How to Replace Post-Conversation Overthinking With Self-Compassion

When you catch yourself replaying a conversation, try this:

- **Pause and reality-check yourself:** Ask: *Did anything truly bad happen? Or is this just my anxiety talking?*
- **Change the channel:** Literally say to yourself: *Nope, we're not doing this.* Then distract yourself—go for a walk, listen to music, do something that shifts your focus.
- **Talk to yourself like you'd talk to a friend:** Would you tell a friend, "Wow, you totally embarrassed yourself in that conversation"? No. So, don't say it to yourself.
- **End every conversation reflection with a positive thought:** Instead of, *Ugh, I was so awkward*, try, *That was a good talk. I showed up as myself, and that's enough.*

You don't need to script, analyze, or perfect your conversations to be a good communicator. You just need to show up as yourself, trust that your words are enough, and let go of the pressure to perform.

Because at the end of the day, connection isn't about saying everything right; it's about being real.

Action Plan—Communication Exercises and Boundary-Setting Strategies

Overthinking steals your confidence, but these exercises will help you retrain your brain to trust yourself. The more you practice intentional communication and boundary-setting, the less energy you'll spend analyzing every interaction. Start small, stay consistent, and remember: You are allowed to take up space in your own life.

Daily Thought-Tracking: Catch and Redirect Overthinking Patterns

Overthinking is often automatic, but with awareness, you can disrupt the cycle. This exercise will help you identify triggers and shift to a more confident mindset.

Step 1: Track your overthinking moments:

- At the end of each day, write down any conversation or decision that caused you to overanalyze.
- Note what specifically triggered your overthinking (e.g.,

fear of judgment, fear of saying the wrong thing, fear of rejection).
- Write down your initial anxious thoughts (e.g., *I probably sounded stupid or I should have said something different*).

Step 2: Reframe the thought:

- Ask yourself: *How much truth is there to this?*
- Challenge it: *Would I judge someone else this harshly?*
- Replace it with a self-compassionate statement (e.g., *I did my best, and people aren't analyzing my words as much as I think*).

Pause and Check-In Strategy for Decision-Making

Many overthinkers say yes too quickly out of guilt or fear of disappointing others. This strategy teaches you to pause and make decisions with intention.

Step 1: Practice the five-second pause: Before responding to a request, take five seconds to check in with yourself. Ask:

- *Do I actually want to do this?*
- *Do I have the energy for this?*
- *Would I be saying yes out of obligation rather than genuine desire?*

Step 2: Use a pre-planned response: If you feel pressure to respond immediately, try saying:

- "Let me check my schedule and get back to you."
- "I need to think about that. I'll let you know soon."
- "I appreciate you asking! I'll see if I can make it work."

This creates space for genuine choice rather than an automatic, people-pleasing response.

Role-Playing Conversations for Confidence Building

Speaking up with confidence takes practice. This exercise helps you rehearse clear, direct communication so it feels natural in real situations.

Option 1: Journal the conversation:

- Choose a situation where you struggle to speak up (e.g., setting a boundary, expressing your needs, or sharing an opinion).
- Write out how you'd typically respond versus how you'd ideally like to respond with confidence.
- Adjust the wording until it feels both assertive and natural.

Option 2: Practice with a friend:

- Ask a trusted friend to role-play with you.
- Practice saying a direct, clear statement without over-explaining (e.g., "I can't take on that extra work right now" instead of "I'm really sorry, I just have so much going on, and I don't want to disappoint anyone").
- Get feedback and adjust accordingly.

Personal Boundary Map Exercise

Defining your boundaries in key areas of life will help you avoid overcommitting and protect your energy. Start with the following:

- **Step 1: Identify key areas for boundaries:** Write down the areas of your life where you need clearer boundaries:
- **Work:** This should include things like limiting after-hours emails and saying no to extra projects.
- **Friendships:** Consider not always being the one to initiate plans and being honest when you need space.
- **Family:** Consider setting limits on discussions that make you uncomfortable and managing expectations around obligations.
- **Dating and relationships:** This should include speaking up about your needs and taking time before responding to emotional demands.
- **Step 2: Define your boundary statements:** For each category, write out a clear boundary statement:
- "I will not answer work emails after 7 p.m."
- "I will not say yes to plans unless I genuinely want to go."
- "I will not justify my choices when setting a boundary with family."
- "I will not apologize for needing time to process my emotions."
- **Step 3: Commit to practicing boundaries:** Each week, choose one boundary to practice enforcing. Reflect on how it feels to honor your own needs without overthinking the impact on others.

Overthinking steals your confidence, but these exercises will help you retrain your brain to trust yourself. The more you practice intentional communication and boundary-setting, the less energy you'll spend analyzing every interaction. Start small, stay consistent, and remember: You are allowed to take up space in your own life.

Final Thoughts

You've come a long way in recognizing and addressing your overthinking tendencies. But the real change happens when you continue applying these strategies in your daily life—not just as a temporary fix but as a long-term approach to healthy, confident communication.

Overthinking may still show up from time to time, but now, you have the tools to redirect it, set boundaries, and trust yourself. The key is consistency. Small, intentional changes build momentum over time, and every step forward strengthens your ability to manage relationships and decisions with ease.

In the next chapter, we'll dive into strategies for maintaining progress, preventing relapse, and creating a long-term mind-set shift. Let's make this confidence and clarity a lasting part of your life!

10

Chapter 10: Your Sustainable Growth Plan

Jane had spent most of her 47 years with a brain that refused to clock out. Whether it was replaying past conversations on a never-ending loop, dissecting every possible meaning behind a one-word text, or catastrophizing a simple work email, she had mastered the art of overthinking. But over the past year, something had changed.

She had gotten serious about breaking the cycle.

Through months of trial and error, she built a personal toolkit— her mental first-aid kit, as she liked to call it. She filled it with things that actually helped: journaling when her thoughts needed a safe space, visualization exercises to stop anxiety mid-spiral, and long, grounding walks in nature where she could breathe deeply and remember that not every problem needed solving right now. And it worked. Well, mostly.

Now, a year in, she faced a new fear: *What if I slip back into old habits?*

She had spent decades overthinking. Would one tough week—one exhausting day, even—send her spiraling back? She knew how easy it was to neglect the habits that had helped her grow. And she also knew herself: If she wasn't careful, she'd start rationalizing bad mental habits the same way she once rationalized staying up until 2 a.m. worrying about a conversation from three days ago. So, Jane made a plan.

She started scheduling regular check-ins with herself. No more waiting until she was knee-deep in a mental hurricane to ask, Hey, are we doing okay? She set aside time every Sunday to reflect:

Where has my mind been this week?

Have I been taking care of myself or just pushing through?

Am I holding onto things I should have let go of by now?

If she noticed any red flags—like an old worry resurfacing or self-doubt creeping in—she'd pause before it took root. Sometimes, that meant journaling it out. Other times, she'd go for a walk, her favorite playlist drowning out the noise in her head.

She also doubled down on self-care—and not just the trendy kind that involved bubble baths and candles (though those had their place). Real self-care. Resting when she was tired, saying no without guilt, and giving herself permission to step away from draining conversations.

Most importantly, she worked on being flexible and kind to herself. Not every week was perfect. Some days, her overthinking still knocked on the door, asking to come inside and unpack its bags. But instead of fighting it or letting it take over, she greeted it like an old acquaintance—*Hey, I see you. But I don't live there anymore.*

One morning, Jane was sipping her coffee when she caught herself overanalyzing a friend's short text. *Is she mad at me? Did I say something wrong?*

She almost laughed. A year ago, this would have hijacked her entire day. But instead of spiraling, she grabbed her journal, wrote down her thoughts, and challenged them: "She's probably just busy. Even if she is upset, I'll ask instead of assuming."

And just like that, the worry lost its grip. That's when Jane realized something huge: She wasn't fixed. She wasn't done with this journey. But she was in control now. And that? That was more than enough.

You've already done the hard work throughout these chapters of recognizing your overthinking patterns and learning how to shift them. Now, let's talk about keeping that progress. The last thing you want is to slip back into the mental spiral every time life gets messy, because it will. This is your long-term roadmap to help you manage overthinking in a way that actually sticks.

Creating a Personal Framework: Your Long-Term Overthinking Strategy

Overthinking isn't just a pesky habit—it's a cycle. And if you've ever found yourself stuck in a loop of analyzing, second-guessing, and worrying about every little detail, you know how exhausting it can be. The key to managing it long-term? A personal framework that helps you navigate those spirals before they take over. This isn't about forcing yourself to "just stop overthinking" (because we both know that doesn't work). It's about creating a structured approach that makes it easier to catch yourself in the act, shift your mindset, and move forward with confidence.

Defining Your Core Values: Your Inner Compass

Let's start with the foundation: What truly matters to you? When you're clear on your core values—the non-negotiable principles that guide your decisions—you don't waste as much time overanalyzing every choice. Instead, your values act like a filter, helping you make decisions with less mental clutter.

Take Lisa's story, for example. Lisa was a chronic overthinker, especially in relationships. Every text message, every minor conflict, every unanswered call sent her into a spiral. But when she identified her core values—honesty, connection, and mutual respect—she realized that she didn't need to stress over whether someone was "mad at her" for taking a few hours to respond. Instead, she could ask herself: *Does this situation align with my values?* If a relationship lacked respect and honesty, it wasn't worth the anxiety. If it did, then she could trust that things were okay.

Let's look at how to define your core values:

- Think of the three to five values that matter most to you. Examples: honesty, personal growth, compassion, stability, adventure.
- Write them down and keep them visible (sticky note on your mirror, lock screen, etc.).
- When faced with a tough decision, ask yourself: *Does this align with my values?* If not, let it go. If yes, move forward confidently.

Setting Specific Goals: Your Roadmap for Change

Without clear goals, managing overthinking feels like swimming in an endless ocean. Setting specific, realistic goals gives you a direction to swim toward. These aren't just "stop overthinking" goals—they're tangible actions that help you retrain your mind.

Meet Miles. Miles always overthought work emails. He'd draft, delete, retype, second-guess, and then stress about whether he should send them at all. It ate up time and drained his confidence. Instead of vaguely telling himself to "be less anxious," he set a clear goal: "Limit myself to three drafts max before sending an email." He also added a time limit: "No more than 10 minutes on a single email." With this structure in place,

Miles had a specific benchmark to follow, which helped cut down his overthinking without making him feel out of control.

So, how do you set effective goals?

- Make them specific and actionable (e.g., "Journal for five minutes when I feel overwhelmed" instead of "Stop over-thinking so much.")
- Set measurable benchmarks (e.g., "Respond to texts within an hour instead of overthinking my reply for days.")
- Start small. Focus on one area at a time (work, relation-ships, decision-making, etc.).

Incorporating Feedback Loops: Tracking Progress and Adjusting

Growth isn't a straight line—it's messy. That's why regular check-ins are crucial to managing overthinking. A feedback loop helps you recognize what's working, what's not, and what needs adjusting before you spiral back into old habits.

Let's talk about Maya. Maya struggled with social anxiety and overthought every conversation. She decided to track her overthinking habits in a journal, writing down:

- What triggered her overthinking?
- How did she respond?
- What helped her move on?

After a month, she noticed patterns: She overthought most

when she was tired or had caffeine. This awareness helped her make small tweaks. She prioritized sleep and cut back on coffee before social events. Over time, her overthinking decreased.

Here are some great ways to create a feedback loop:

- **Weekly self-check-ins:** Ask yourself, *Where did I overthink this week? What helped? What didn't?*
- **Use a journal or notes app:** Track patterns in your thoughts and behaviors.
- **Invite external feedback:** Ask trusted friends/mentors for observations (e.g., "Have I seemed more present and decisive lately?").
- **Adjust as needed:** If a strategy isn't working, tweak it rather than abandon it.

Your personal framework isn't a rigid plan—it's a living, evolving strategy that helps you manage overthinking on your terms. By defining your core values, setting specific goals, and incorporating feedback loops, you create a sustainable system that makes overthinking easier to catch and manage over time. No more exhausting mental spirals. No more getting lost in "what-ifs." Just a clear, structured way to think less and live more.

Long-Term Maintenance: Staying Mindful and Intentional

Managing overthinking isn't a one-and-done deal. It's a long game—one that requires awareness, small adjustments, and the occasional pat on the back (seriously, you deserve that). The progress you've made is real, but without intentional effort, old habits have a sneaky way of creeping back in. That's why long-term maintenance matters. Think of it like keeping a garden—if you don't check in, pull weeds, and nourish what's growing, the overthinking vines will take over again. So, let's set up a system that keeps your progress intact without feeling like yet another thing to stress about.

Regular Check-Ins: Keep Yourself on Track

Just like a good friend checks in on you, you need to check in on yourself. Regularly evaluating where you're at prevents overthinking from creeping back in unnoticed. Think of it as a course correction—small adjustments to keep you moving in the right direction instead of waking up one day wondering, *How did I end up in the overthinking spiral again?*

Noah used to agonize over every conversation, replaying them in his head and analyzing what he *should have* said. He made great progress by practicing mindfulness and setting boundaries with his thoughts. But after a stressful work period, he found himself slipping back into the habit. Instead of panicking, he used a simple self-check-in:

· *Am I overanalyzing conversations again?*
· *What's causing it?*
· *What helped me before, and can I apply that now?*

Because Noah had built the habit of checking in with himself weekly, he caught the backslide early and course-corrected before it got overwhelming.

So, how can you build regular check-ins?

- **Set a reminder:** Weekly or monthly, ask yourself *Am I overthinking more lately?*
- **Journal or voice memo it:** A quick reflection on what's working (or what's not) can be eye-opening.
- **Buddy system:** Find a friend who's working on their own mental habits and check in with each other.

The goal isn't perfection—it's awareness. Checking in keeps you in charge of your progress instead of letting old patterns creep back unnoticed.

Celebrating Milestones: Recognizing Your Wins

Here's a secret: Your brain loves rewards. The more you acknowledge your growth, the more likely you are to keep going. Overthinking can make you overlook progress (*I'm still overthinking sometimes, so have I really improved?*), but celebrating milestones—big or small—reinforces the fact that, YES, you *are* making strides.

Maya used to spiral into self-doubt every time she had to make a decision. After months of actively practicing trusting her choices, she caught herself making a decision in under a minute—without panicking. That was huge for her! Instead of brushing it off, she took herself out for coffee to celebrate.

Guess what? Her brain associated that positive reinforcement with progress, making it easier to keep going.

Let's check out some ways to celebrate your progress:

- **Create a wins list:** Write down every time you notice yourself managing overthinking better.
- **Reward yourself:** Treat yourself when you hit a milestone (*Didn't overanalyze that text? Hello, fancy latte!*).
- **Tell someone:** Share your progress with a supportive friend who will cheer you on.

Your growth deserves recognition. Celebrating keeps you motivated and reinforces the fact that you *are* making a difference in your own life.

Adjusting Goals as Needed: Staying Flexible

Life changes. And that means your goals need to, too. What worked when you started might not be as effective later on, and that's okay. Being flexible with your goals keeps them relevant, realistic, and helpful.

Julia started her overthinking recovery by setting a goal to stop rereading every email five times before sending it. She succeeded! But then, her anxiety started showing up in a new way—she began second-guessing big life decisions instead. Instead of feeling like she had failed, she adjusted her focus to tackle this new challenge.

199

Being flexible with your goals isn't about giving up—it's about evolving.

Here's how you can adjust your goals:

- **Ask, *Is this goal still relevant?*** If your main struggle has shifted, update your focus.
- **Modify, don't scrap:** Instead of dropping a goal entirely, tweak it to match where you are now.
- **Be kind to yourself:** Growth isn't linear. Setbacks don't erase progress; they just mean it's time for an adjustment.

Staying mindful and intentional isn't about never overthinking again—it's about catching yourself sooner, bouncing back faster, and celebrating the progress you've made. With regular check-ins, celebrating milestones, and adjusting your goals as life evolves, you'll have the tools to keep moving forward—even when life throws its inevitable curveballs.

Overthinking might have been your default for years, but it doesn't have to be your future. With the right approach, you can maintain your progress, trust your choices, and step into a life with way less mental clutter.

Tools to Avoid Slipping Back Into Overthinking

You've put in the work, made progress, and gained control over your overthinking tendencies. But let's be real—old habits have a sneaky way of creeping back in when you least expect them. A stressful day, an unexpected conflict, or even just being overtired can trigger that familiar spiral of *What if...?* and *Did I say the wrong thing?* The good news? You don't have to fall back into old patterns. By developing a proactive strategy, you can recognize the warning signs early, use alternative coping tools, and strengthen your support system to keep yourself on track.

Recognizing Your Overthinking Warning Signs

Overthinking doesn't just happen—it has patterns. The key to staying ahead of it is recognizing your personal triggers and warning signs before they pull you into a full-blown spiral. If you can catch overthinking early, it's way easier to disrupt it.

Marcus used to overanalyze every decision at work, from sending emails to speaking up in meetings. He got better at managing it, but one day, he caught himself staring at an email for 15 minutes and rewriting the same sentence five times. That was his cue that he was slipping into old habits. Because he had identified his patterns, he was able to stop himself and move forward before getting trapped in analysis paralysis.

Exercise: Your Overthinking Self-Assessment Checklist

Check the signs that apply to you:
  ☐ I catch myself rereading texts, emails, or messages multiple times before sending.
  ☐ I ask for reassurance more than usual ("Do you think I handled that okay?").

☐ I replay past conversations in my head and analyze them.

☐ I struggle to make simple decisions (*What should I order? Which movie should I watch?*).

☐ I feel mentally exhausted from overanalyzing things that *should* be straightforward.

If you checked more than two, it's time to pause and reset before the spiral gains momentum.

Building an Emotional Regulation Toolkit

Overthinking is often a response to emotional discomfort—an attempt to create certainty or control when things feel unpredictable. The trick? Instead of thinking your way out of uncertainty, feel your way through it with emotional regulation techniques.

Olivia had a tendency to overthink every social interaction. She'd overanalyze tone, wording, and nonverbal cues, trying to predict what others thought of her. When she started practicing emotional regulation—deep breathing, movement, and self-soothing techniques—she found that her need to overthink decreased naturally because she was managing the underlying emotions before they spiraled.

Exercise: Disrupt the Spiral

Next time you notice yourself overthinking, try one of these physical or mental interventions:

Physically reset your brain:

· Move! Stand up, stretch, shake out your hands. Physical movement can shift your thought patterns.
· Place your hand on your heart and take five slow breaths. This signals safety to your nervous system.
· Change environments—step outside, switch rooms, or do a quick walk.

Mentally disrupt the thought pattern:

· Say "STOP" out loud. It interrupts the loop.
· Ask yourself: *Will this still matter in a week? A month? A year?*
· Set a timer for five minutes: Allow yourself to overthink, but once the timer goes off, move on.

Accountability and Support Systems

Overthinking thrives in isolation. The more time you spend alone in your head, the easier it is for small worries to snowball into overwhelming doubts. That's why building a solid support system is crucial—it helps keep you grounded, challenged, and reminded that you don't have to figure everything out alone.

Cory used to handle stress alone, which made overthinking worse. But once he built a support system—a therapist, a mentor at work, and a close friend who gently called him out when he was spiraling—he found it easier to stay accountable. Having someone to check in with stopped him from getting

203

lost in his own thoughts.

Exercise: Your Relationship Inventory

Take a moment to evaluate your current support system:

- **Who in my life actively supports my growth?** (Friends, family, therapist, mentor, coach, online community?)
- **Who unintentionally feeds my overthinking?** (*Do I have a friend who encourages overanalyzing instead of helping me move forward?*)
- **Who can I turn to when I need grounding or perspective?** (*Do I have someone who helps me refocus when I spiral?*)

If your current circle doesn't feel supportive enough, consider expanding it:

- Find a therapist, coach, or mentor for guidance.
- Join a community or group that encourages personal growth.
- Build friendships with people who help you stay present and intentional.

Overthinking might have been your default for years, but you are not powerless against it. By recognizing your early warning signs, using emotional regulation tools, and surrounding yourself with the proper support, you can stop overthinking before it takes over again.

The goal isn't to never have anxious thoughts—it's to catch

them early, manage them effectively, and move forward with confidence. And guess what? You've already proven that you *can* do this. Now, you just have to keep going.

Action Plan: A Customizable Plan to Ensure Lasting Change

Overcoming overthinking isn't just about breaking bad habits— it's about building a life that supports mental clarity and confidence. And to do that, you need a strategy that actually fits your life. A plan that feels doable, adaptable, and sustainable— not some overwhelming checklist that makes you feel like you're failing before you even start.

This chapter is about creating a personal roadmap to ensure your progress *sticks.* No more falling into the trap of "I'll work on this later." No more feeling lost when challenges arise. You're designing a plan that helps you keep growing, celebrating wins, and adjusting when necessary. Ready? Let's build it.

Building Your Personal Growth Roadmap

Big changes happen through small, intentional steps. Instead of trying to "fix" everything at once, focus on daily, man- ageable actions that create lasting shifts in your mindset and behavior.

Alex used to get stuck in "analysis paralysis" every time they

205

had to make a decision. Instead of telling themselves to just be more decisive (which never worked), they broke it down into small, realistic steps:

- **Week 1:** Set a 30-second timer to make small decisions (what to eat, what to wear).
- **Week 2:** When second-guessing, ask: *What would I tell a friend in this situation?*
- **Week 3:** Practice making one decision a day without asking for outside opinions.
- **Week 4:** Celebrate progress and adjust strategies if needed.

Small steps create momentum, making change manageable and sustainable.

Exercise: Your Next 30 Days

Create a customizable goal-setting worksheet for the next month:

1. **Pick one focus area:** It could be decision-making, letting go of past mistakes, managing social anxiety, etc.
2. **Set a small daily habit:** For example, "Spend 5 minutes journaling instead of overanalyzing" or "Pause before seeking reassurance."
3. **Weekly check-in question:** What's working? What needs adjusting?
4. **Reward yourself for progress:** "If I stick to this for two weeks, I'll treat myself to a self-care day."

Write this plan down somewhere visible (journal, notes app, sticky note on your mirror) to keep yourself accountable!

Tracking Your Wins and Learning From Setbacks

Progress isn't linear. You'll have wins, and you'll have setbacks. Both are part of growth. The key is to acknowledge your progress and learn from missteps—without beating yourself up.

Jess was doing great at managing overthinking—until a tough week at work sent her spiraling. Instead of seeing it as proof of failure, she looked at what happened:

- She realized she hadn't been sleeping well.
- She noticed she was skipping her daily walks (which usually helped her clear her mind).
- She adjusted her plan by prioritizing rest and movement before diving into "fixing" her overthinking.

Learning from setbacks isn't about punishing yourself—it's about using them as data to refine your approach.

Exercise: Celebrate and Adjust Log

Create a weekly reflection practice to track your wins and tweak your strategies:

- **Write down one thing you did well this week:**
- Example: "I didn't overanalyze a conversation that usually

207

would have stressed me out!"
- **Write down one challenge you faced:**
- Example: "I caught myself replaying an awkward moment over and over."
- **Ask,** *What can I learn from this?*
- Example: "I tend to overthink more when I'm exhausted. I need to prioritize sleep."

Tracking wins and setbacks keeps you motivated and adaptable, so you can keep moving forward without guilt.

Committing to Growth as a Lifelong Practice

There's no finish line to personal growth—and that's a good thing. You don't have to be "fully healed" to enjoy life, make decisions, and trust yourself. Growth is about progress, not perfection. The key is to keep moving forward, adjusting as needed, and treating yourself with patience along the way.

Danielle used to think she needed to "fix" herself before she could fully relax in relationships. But over time, she realized growth isn't about becoming someone different—it's about becoming more of who she already is. She committed to lifelong self-improvement without the pressure to be perfect.

Exercise: Write a Letter to Your Future Self

Take five minutes to write a letter to yourself six months from now:

1. **Start with encouragement:** "Hey [your name], I know you're working hard on trusting yourself more. I'm proud of you for even reading this."
2. **Acknowledge progress:** "Right now, you're focusing on [your main goal]. It's not always easy, but you've already come so far."
3. **Remind yourself to be flexible:** "There might be setbacks, and that's okay. What matters is that you keep going."
4. **End with a vision of who you're becoming:** "I know you'll be stronger, calmer, and more confident six months from now. No matter where you are in the journey, I believe in you."

Seal it, set a reminder to open it in six months, and let yourself be surprised by how much you've grown.

A lasting mindset shift doesn't happen overnight—it happens through small, consistent changes that become second nature over time. By creating a personalized roadmap, tracking your progress with self-compassion, and committing to lifelong growth, you'll build a sustainable strategy for overcoming overthinking for good.

And remember—you're already on your way. Each small step you take is proof that you're capable of real, lasting change. Keep going.

11

Conclusion

Throughout this book, we've explored the ways overthinking sneaks into our lives—how it hijacks our relationships, our careers, and even our ability to make a simple decision. But more importantly, we've uncovered the strategies to break free from it.

Remember Melissa from Chapter !? She thought she was just an overthinker at work but soon realized that her constant analysis and self-doubt seeped into her relationship, leaving her feeling disconnected. Through self-discovery, she learned to recognize when she was spiraling and replace those old habits with new, productive thought patterns. Then there was Jeremy in Chapter 3, whose overthinking created stress and tension in his marriage. When it ended, he faced a hard truth—his mind had been sabotaging his connection all along. But instead of dwelling in regret, he found healing in nature, grounding himself through hiking whenever those thoughts tried to pull him under. And let's not forget Macy in Chapter 8, who spent two years stuck in engagement limbo because decision fatigue kept her paralyzed. She and her fiancé sought help, faced their fears, and finally took action, proving that clarity comes when we step forward, not when we sit in indecision.

And then, of course, there's my story. In the introduction, I told you about the time I found myself boarding a plane alone. I was supposed to be with my girlfriend, but instead, I spiraled into an abyss of self-doubt, wondering what I had done wrong, what I could have changed, and what was wrong with me. I didn't know it then, but life was already writing me a better chapter. It took time, but I learned the truth: while we're busy overthinking one chapter, life is already preparing the next one for us. We just have to stop overthinking long enough to turn the page.

So, what's your next chapter?

Now that you've worked through this book, you have the tools to quiet the noise and take action. You've seen how small, consistent steps create real change. Whether it's calming your mind, making a difficult decision, or stepping into the unknown, you're no longer just thinking about it; you're ready to act.

Perfection is never the goal. Growth is. And you've already started.

If this book has helped you in any way, I'd love to hear from you. Leaving a review not only helps me as an author, but it also helps others who might be feeling stuck in the same cycle of overthinking find the guidance they need.

And if you're ready to take this work even deeper, check out my first book, *Letting Go Right Now*, where I explore how to release what no longer serves you and create space for what truly matters.

Your mind is clear. Your next chapter is waiting. Now go live it.

Thanks and Feedback

Thank you for reading "The Practical Path to Stop Overthinking & Fix Your Relationships."

As an author and indie publisher, I truly appreciate your reading my book. I hope this experience supports your growth and opens your life to positive growth and happy relationships.

If you have 60 seconds and have not already left a review on Amazon, it would mean the world to me to hear your honest feedback. It does wonders for the book, and I love hearing about your experience with it.

To leave your feedback please visit my book's page on Amazon page where you can leave your review.

Once again, thank you for reading and feedback.

With gratitude,
    Matt

Bonus Content

I have created valuable bonus content to support your journey with "The Practical Guide to Stop Overthinking & Fix Your Relationships."

Using the QR code below will take you to a site where you can claim your bonuses.

The bonus content includes:

- **21-Day Overthinking Reset Challenge** - Experience calmer thoughts and deeper connection in just minutes a day (alone or with your partner)
- **Proven Relationship Communication Scripts** - End misunderstandings and resolve conflicts with confidence using word-for-word conversation guides
- **Overthinking Emergency Kit** - Get immediate relief from anxiety spirals and racing thoughts in 5 minutes or less

To collect your bonuses:

- Open your camera app.
- Point your mobile device at the QR code that follows.
- This will take you to a landing page where you can claim

your bonuses.

Or you can go to this link in your web browser:

https://subscribepage.io/FTtkeb

I hope you find this content useful in your personal journey to let go and I wish you every success.

About the Author

Accomplished author Matt Tomporowski writes transformative self-help books and his blog, *Chasing Dreams in Middle Life*, to support readers in their emotional well-being and personal development. His mission is to help readers lead happy and healthy lives.

Through his writing, he enables people to break free from limiting patterns and beliefs, guiding them toward happiness and fulfillment. His approach combines clinical research with practical, accessible strategies for lasting change. Matt's work aims to help others release emotional baggage and create lives filled with purpose and joy.

Join Matt on his ongoing journey and discover more insights on his Substack blog "Chasing Dreams in Middle Life" at https://matttomporowski.substack.com/

Also by Matt Tomporowski

"LETTING GO RIGHT NOW"

The breakthrough guide to clearing your mind and eliminating negative thinking.

Are you ready to break free from what's holding you back?

In "Letting Go Right Now," Matt Tomporowski shares practical wisdom, science-backed techniques, and actionable strategies to help readers:

· Clear their minds of persistent negative thoughts

- Release emotional attachments that no longer serve them
- Develop powerful mindfulness practices for daily life
- Create an action plan for moving forward with confidence
- Transform how they respond to life's challenges

This easy-to-read guide combines inspiration, scientific insights, and step-by-step exercises designed to help individuals overcome what's holding them back and embrace a more fulfilling life.

Available now in print, e-book, and audiobook formats.

Scan the QR code below or visit https://mybook.to/Letting_Go_Right_Now to learn more about "Letting Go Right Now" on Amazon.

References

Alouani, N. (2021, May 10). *Dark Bezos' 70% rule will help you decide faster.* Big Self. https://medium.com/big-self-society/dark-bezoss-70-rule-will-help-you-decide-faster-b9bc1c9c4168

Ankrom, S. (2024, February 5). *How to stop constant worrying about the future.* Verywell Mind. https://www.verywellmind.com/are-you-worrying-too-much-2584124

Black, D. S., & Slavich, G. M. (2016). Mindfulness meditation and the immune system: a systematic review of randomized controlled trials. *Annals of the New York Academy of Sciences, 1373*(1), 13–24. https://doi.org/10.1111/nyas.12998

Camacho, B. (2024, February 28). *Why do I overthink everything? A psychiatrist explains.* Talkiatry. https://www.talkiatry.com/blog/why-do-i-overthink-everything

Cherry, K. (2024, May 17). *How neuroplasticity works.* Verywell Mind. https://www.verywellmind.com/what-is-brain-plasticity-2794886

Cirino, E. (2024, June 6). *12 tips to help you stop ruminating.* Healthline. https://www.healthline.com/health/how-to-stop-ruminating

Clarke, J. (2023, November 27). *What is analysis paralysis?* Verywell Mind. https://www.verywellmind.com/what-is-a nalysis-paralysis-5223790

Desbordes, G., Negi, L. T., Pace, T. W. W., Wallace, B. A., Raison, C. L., & Schwartz, E. L. (2012). Effects of mindful-attention and compassion meditation training on amygdala response to emotional stimuli in an ordinary, non-meditative state. *Frontiers in Human Neuroscience, 6*(1). https://doi.org/10.33 89/fnhum.2012.00292

Ezzat Obaya, H., Ali, A., Salem, A. M., Ali Shehata, M., Aldhahi, M. I., Muka, T., Marqués-Sulé, E., Taha, M. E., Gaber, M. A., & Atef, H. (2023). Effect of aerobic exercise, slow deep breathing and mindfulness meditation on cortisol and glucose levels in women with type 2 diabetes mellitus: a randomized controlled trial. *Frontiers in Physiology, 14.* https://doi.org/10.3389/fphys. 2023.1186546

Holland, K. (2023, March 16). *Amygdala hijack: When emotion takes over.* Healthline. https://www.healthline.com/health/str ess/amygdala-hijack

Jermann, F., Cordera, P., Carlei, C., Weber, B., Baggio, S., Bon-dolfi, G., & Cervena, K. (2024). Impact of mindfulness-based stress reduction on sleep-related parameters in a community sample. *Advances in Integrative Medicine, 11*(4), 273–279. https://doi.org/10.1016/j.aimed.2024.08.005

Jordan, R. (2015, June 30). *Stanford researchers find mental health prescription: Nature | Stanford Report*. News.stanford.edu. https://news.stanford.edu/stories/2015/06/hiking-mental-health-063015

Laderer, A. (2024, January 19). *5 vagus nerve exercises to help you chill out*. Charlie Health. https://www.charliehealth.com/post/vagus-nerve-exercises

Lamothe, C. (2024, July 3). *How to stop overthinking: 14 strategies*. Healthline. https://www.healthline.com/health/how-to-stop-overthinking

Ligeza, T. S., Maciejczyk, M., Wyczesany, M., & Junghofer, M. (2022). The effects of a single aerobic exercise session on mood and neural emotional reactivity in depressed and healthy young adults: A late positive potential study. *Psychophysiology*, *60*(1). https://doi.org/10.1111/psyp.14137

Meek, W. (2024, February 26). *How generalized anxiety disorder affects memory*. Verywell Mind. https://www.verywellmind.com/anxiety-and-memory-1393133

Mindfulness meditation. (n.d.). John Hopkins Medicine. https://www.hopkinsmedicine.org/health/wellness-and-prevention/mindfulness-meditation

Nwanedo, E. (2021, July 21). *How to find balance between thinking and emotion*. Medium; Change Your Mind Change Your Life. https://medium.com/change-your-mind/how-to-find-balance-between-thinking-and-emotion-936f0d1f1c7b

Oh, V. K. S., Sarwar, A., & Pervez, N. (2022). The study of mindfulness as an intervening factor for enhanced psychological well-being in building the level of resilience. *Figshare.com*, *13*(1). https://doi.org/10.3389/fpsyg.2022.1056834

Pekovic, R. (2019, October 17). *What are some exercises to improve decision making?* Quora. https://www.quora.com/What-are-some-exercises-to-improve-decision-making

Powell, A. (2018, April 9). *Harvard researchers study how mindfulness may change the brain in depressed patients.* Harvard Gazette. https://news.harvard.edu/gazette/story/2018/04/harvard-researchers-study-how-mindfulness-may-change-the-brain-in-depressed-patients

Raypole, C. (2020, November 13). *Emotional triggers: Definition and how to manage them.* Healthline. https://www.healthline.com/health/mental-health/emotional-triggers

Raypole, C. (2023, March 29). *Physical symptoms of anxiety: How does it feel?* Healthline. https://www.healthline.com/health/physical-symptoms-of-anxiety

Reid, S. (2022, July 6). *Setting healthy boundaries in relationships.* HelpGuide. https://www.helpguide.org/relationships/socialconnection/setting-healthy-boundaries-in-relationships

Serotonin. (2022, March 18). Cleveland Clinic. https://my.clevelandclinic.org/health/articles/22572-serotonin

Sutton, J. (2024, February 2). *18 effective thought-stopping techniques.* PositivePsychology. https://positivepsychology .com/thought-stopping-techniques/

Techniques to help activate your parasympathetic nervous system. (2021, January 19). East Sussex Osteopaths. https://www.easts ussex-osteopaths.co.uk/2021/01/19/activate-your-parasympa thetic-nervous-system-with-these-simple-techniques/

Tindle, J., & Tadi, P. (2022, October 31). *Neuroanatomy, parasym- pathetic nervous system.* PubMed. https://www.ncbi.nlm.nih.go v/books/NBK553141/

Tomporowski, M. (2025, January 25). How overthinking nearly ruined my epic world adventure (and what saved me). Substack.com; *Chasing Dreams in Middle Life.* https://matttom porowski.substack.com/p/how-overthinking-nearly-ruined- my?r=fk82p&utm_campaign=post&utm_medium=web&tried Redirect=true

Victor, D. (2023, November 21). *How music can reduce stress and improve mental health.* Harmony & Healing. https://www.harm onyandhealing.org/how-music-can-reduce-stress/

Wilson, S. J., Syed, S. U., Yang, I. S., & Cole, S. W. (2024). A tale of two marital stressors: Comparing proinflammatory responses to partner distress and marital conflict. *Brain Behavior and Immunity, 119,* 898–907. https://doi.org/10.1016/j.bbi.2024.05. 003

Winch, G. (2013, June 18). *10 signs that you might have fear of failure.* Psychology Today. https://www.psychologytoday.com/

ca/blog/the-squeaky-wheel/201306/10-signs-that-you-mig ht-have-fear-of-failure

Yasir, M. (2023, September 30). *The art of observing and not absorbing*. Medium. https://medium.com/@maria13.ria/the-a rt-of-observing-and-not-absorbing-73c8f52ada1

Made in the USA
Middletown, DE
30 April 2025

74976352R00128